Pocket-guide to Southern African BIRDS

Burger Cillié
Ulrich Oberprieler

SUNBIRD
PUBLISHING

Contents

Second edition 2002 Sunbird Publishing
ISBN 0 624 04075 5
10 9 8 7 6 5

First edition published by J.L. van Schaik Publishers

Cover design by Elaine du Toit
Cover photograph by Nico Myburgh
Illustrations by Anneliese Burger
Reproduction by The Future Group, Centurion
Printed and bound by Tien Wah Press, Singapore

Introduction

This booklet has been designed to fit into a shirt pocket and be carried along into the field. Its user-friendly layout and easy method of identifying a new bird make it a must, especially for people who have just started to watch birds.

Most nature lovers, particularly hikers who regularly wish to consult a bird guide, will appreciate this book's light and compact design. It is the ideal book for birdwatchers who do not wish to be burdened with larger and heavier books.

More than 420 of the more common birds of southern Africa (south of the Cunene and Zambezi) are listed. In order to simplify identification, the rarer birds have been omitted; it is seldom that the user will encounter a bird not inluded in this book.

The birds have been divided into 12 logical groups according to externally visible characteristics. These are discussed in the section "Key to the major groups of birds". This system, which is linked to colour codes throughout the book, and the abbreviated alphabetical index in the back of the book, aid the user in quickly finding the bird to be identified.

The relative size, principal habitat, food, social structure and nest type of each bird are indicated by means of symbols as described in the section "Symbols".

The colour photographs have been chosen to illustrate the important characteristics of each bird. Smaller photographs show the differences between the adult male and the immature, female or non-breeding bird where appropriate.

In accordance with current practice, the more specific name such as "African Fish Eagle" or "Southern Red Bishop" has been used, instead of simply "Fish Eagle" or "Red Bishop". This is in order to avoid confusion with similar species in other parts of the world.

This pocket guide is a compact but well illustrated identification booklet that many birdwatchers will find indispensable.

Symbols and abbreviations on photographs

Ad	Adult	Imm	Immature
Br	Breeding	Nbr	Non-breeding
♂	Male	♀	Female

Different parts of a bird's body

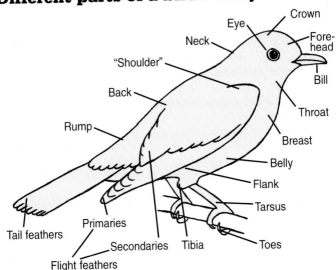

Vegetation map

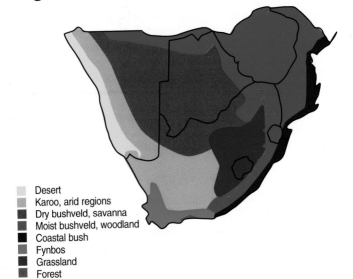

Desert
Karoo, arid regions
Dry bushveld, savanna
Moist bushveld, woodland
Coastal bush
Fynbos
Grassland
Forest

Key to the major groups of birds

As there are more than 420 birds described in this pocket guide, many birdwatchers will not know where to start searching for a particular species. The birds are therefore divided into a number of major groups (marked with colour codes) according to their visual characteristics. The following key will help you to recognise these major groups of birds. Follow the key step by step. Study each group and eliminate groups as you go along, until you reach the group that describes the main characteristics of the bird that you wish to identify.

Use the colour codes to quickly find the different groups in the pocket guide

1. Flying waterbirds

Waterbirds that fly or dive from the air into the water: long, narrow wings; mostly white; larger than a dove. (pp. 8–11)

2. Swimming and diving waterbirds

Waterbirds that swim or dive from the surface: webbed or lobed toes; larger than a dove. (pp. 12–20)

3. Larger wading birds

Long legs; mostly close to water, but some also in grass-veld, arid regions and bushveld; fowl-sized or larger. (pp. 21–32)

4. Smaller waders

Long legs; mostly close to water, but some also in grassveld and arid regions; fowl-sized or smaller. (pp. 33–43)

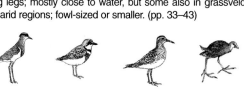

1

5. Fowl-like birds (gamebirds)

Ground-living; brown plumage (except guineafowl); dove-sized or larger. (pp. 44–49)

6. Birds of prey (raptors)

Hooked bills; sharp claws; excellent eyesight; active by day or night. (pp. 50–64)

7. Fruiteaters

Robust and broad bills; crow-sized or smaller. (pp. 65–69)

8. Birds with long, straight bills

Occur near water or in trees; dove-sized or smaller. (pp. 70–74)

9. Birds with long, decurved bills

Crow-sized or smaller. (pp. 75–84)

10. Aerial insectivores

Catch insects in flight; long, narrow and pointed wings; small, triangular bills; dove-sized or smaller. (pp. 85–90)

11. Insectivores

Thrush-like bills: upper jaw slightly decurved or hooked at the tip.

a. Stout bills

Birds crow-sized or smaller. (pp. 91–98)

b. Medium-sized bills

Birds dove-sized or smaller (except some cuckoos). (pp. 99–126)

c. Tiny bills

Birds about sparrow-sized or smaller. (pp. 127–133)

12. Seedeaters

Doves and pigeons, and finch-like birds with short, conical bills. (pp. 134–153)

Symbols

The following characteristics of birds are indicated by means of symbols: (The symbols in each block are arranged in order of importance.)

Size

The size of each bird (indicated by a dark silhouette) is compared to one of three well-known birds (indicated in red):

 Cape Sparrow 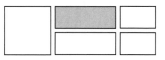 Cape Turtle Dove Helmeted Guineafowl

Habitat

A habitat is the type of country in which the bird will live and occur. There are similarities between the habitat and the vegetation zones as indicated on the map on page (iv). A specific habitat may, however, be found within a vegetation zone.

Towns, cities and gardens
These areas vary from the centre of a metropolitan region to the gardens of farm houses.

Freshwater areas
These are dams, vleis, marshes, pans, rivers and streams. The shores may be open beaches, rocks or beds of reeds and sedges.

Marine areas
The coastline, inshore areas and the open ocean are included in this habitat. Estuaries are transition zones between marine and freshwater areas.

Mountains and hills
High mountains support a unique avifauna. The birds of smaller hills and koppies are similar to those of the adjacent country.

Fynbos
The Cape fynbos is well known, but high mountains may also be covered in fynbos-like vegetation.

Deserts, arid country and dry scrub
The Karoo, Namib, Namaqualand and Bushmanland are typical of this habitat.

Grassland
Grassland includes not only open grasslands, but also smaller patches of grass within other vegetation zones.

Trees and thickets
Thornveld, savanna, bushveld, woodland and even thickets in other vegetation zones form this habitat. Dense riverine bush is a transition zone to forests.

Evergreen forests and coastal bush
Forests constitute a dense vegetation type where the canopies of trees form a continuous layer. Inland forest trees are usually tall, while coastal bush consists of smaller trees.

Widespread
Some birds occur in a variety of habitats. Their preferred habitat is indicated.

Food

The main food sources of every bird species are indicated, but birds will from time to time also take other food.

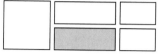

Seeds
The most utilized seeds are those of grasses, although birds will also feed on the seeds of other plants.

Fruit and berries
Fruit and berries are usually seasonal. For this reason fruit-eating birds also need to take other food.

Nectar
Nectar is produced in the base of a flower. As it is not particularly nutritious, birds supplement their diet with other food.

Vegetation: leaves, grass and flowers
Few birds have a digestive system capable of dealing with tough plant material. Softer parts are usually preferred.

Plankton
Plankton are microscopically small organisms in water. A special filter mechanism is needed to utilize this food.

Insects and other terrestrial invertebrates
Insects, spiders, scorpions, worms and other invertebrates living on land are eaten by many birds.

Crabs, snails and other aquatic invertebrates
A large variety of invertebrates living in water form an important food source for many birds.

Fish and frogs
Some birds feed on both fish and frogs, while others either take fish only, or feed on frogs and tadpoles.

Carrion
Dead animals, large and small, are considered to be carrion.

Birds
Adult birds and chicks are prey for other birds.

Small mammals and reptiles
Mice, rats, dassies and hares are examples of small mammals. The important reptiles utilized as a food source are snakes and lizards.

Omnivores
Omnivores utilize a wide variety of food, including both animal and plant material.

Sociability
The most prevalent social structure of every bird species is indicated.

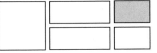

Solitary
Is usually found on its own.

Pairs
The male and female are usually seen together.

Family groups or small flocks
Groups of less than about a dozen individuals.

Large flocks
Groups varying from about a dozen to thousands of individuals.

Nests
Most birds build nests for breeding. The figure in this block indicates the average number of eggs per clutch. The following nest structures are indicated:

None **No nest**
The eggs are laid on the ground, a ledge or other suitable place, such as the nest of other birds.

Scrape in the ground
A simple hollow which may or may not be lined with nesting material.

Heap
A turret of mud or soil on which the eggs are laid.

Platform
A flat structure of branches, twigs or other plant material.

Saucer
A flat structure with a slight rim, usually built of plant material.

Cup
A deep cup or bowl-shaped structure, usually built of plant material.

Burrow in an earth bank or in the ground
The eggs are laid in a chamber at the end of a tunnel. This burrow may be self-excavated or dug by another animal.

Cavity in a tree
Cavities in trees may be self-excavated. Birds also often use natural cavities or those left by other animals. The nest may or may not be lined.

Neatly woven nest
Typical of the weavers. These nests are usually suspended at the tips of slender branches, or built among reeds and sedges.

Round or oval nests of plant material
Although also woven, these nests appear untidy.

Unique
Unique nest
Some birds have unique nests which are described in the text.

Parasite
Nesting parasite
The eggs are laid in the nest of a host who will incubate them and rear the chicks.

Migratory patterns

The migratory pattern of each bird is indicated on the distribution map by means of three different colours: (The figure below each map is the species' southern African number.)

Resident
Breeds here and occurs in southern Africa throughout the year.

Summer resident
Breeds in southern Africa during the summer months (October–April), but migrates north in winter, usually to other parts of Africa.

Visitor
Found in southern Africa during the summer months (October–April), but migrates north by the end of summer to breed, usually in Eurasia. Pelagic seabirds breeding in Antarctica occur along our coast during the winter months.

Group 1: Flying waterbirds

Waterbirds which fly over the water and sometimes dive into the water from the air are mostly associated with the sea, although some of them occur on inland waters. These are the **albatrosses**, the **petrels**, the **gulls**, the **terns** and the **gannets**. They have long, narrow wings which are well suited for effortless gliding flight. Their white plumage helps to camouflage them when seen from the water.
The **albatrosses** and **petrels** are birds of the open ocean and are seldom seen inshore. They often follow ships and fishing boats.
Gulls and **terns** are inshore birds, but also occur on fresh water. Gulls, with their strong bills, hooked at the tip, are well adapted for a scavenging lifestyle. Terns have long pointed wings, making them excellent fliers and enabling them to dive into the water or take food from the surface.
Gannets fish by plunging into the water. They are gregarious birds, not only when breeding, but also while feeding.

Black-browed Albatross

Resembles a large Kelp Gull with long narrow wings, but the bill is yellow with a pink tip. The white underwing has a broad black edge. The immature bird has a grey head and bill; it may be confused with other albatrosses. It croaks when fighting for food. Common during winter over the open ocean, but also seen in coastal waters. Large numbers gather around trawlers to feed on offal.
(Swartrugmalmok)

12

Ant-arctic

Pintado Petrel

A pied petrel. The underparts are white, the throat black. The upperparts and wings are black with white patches. Common during winter over the open ocean, especially near trawlers. After stormy weather it may be seen along the coast. Settles on the water to feed. Paddles with the feet to bring food to the surface or dives for it. Alternates flapping and gliding flight.
(Seeduifstormvoël)

21

Ant-arctic

Kelp Gull

A large gull with a black back and wings. The adult has dark eyes, a yellow bill with a red spot at the tip and green-grey legs. (The uncommon Lesser Blackbacked Gull has yellow eyes and legs.) The immature is speckled dark brown and could be confused with the rarer skuas. Found commonly along the coast, especially in harbours. Follows trawlers in search of offal.
(Swartrugmeeu)   312

Grey-headed Gull

The pale yellow eyes and bright red bill distinguish the adult from Hartlaub's Gull. Breeding birds have grey heads. Non-breeding birds have grey patches behind the eyes, but their bills are still redder than those of Hartlaub's Gull. Immatures have dark eyes and orange bills and legs. Found along the coast as well as on larger inland waters. Breeds in colonies.
(Gryskopmeeu)
                                             315

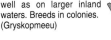

Hartlaub's Gull

Characteristic are the dark eyes and white head. When breeding, the head is pale grey. Could then be confused with the Grey-headed Gull which, however, has yellow eyes and a bright red bill. Immatures have brown bills and legs. Occurs along the West Coast (seldom over the open ocean) and adjacent inland. Scavenges along the coast or around trawlers. Breeds in colonies on islands or buildings during winter.   (Hartlaubse meeu)
                                             316

Imm

Ad

Cape Gannet

Unmistakable. A large white bird with black tips to the wings and tail. The head and neck are yellow, patterned with black; the bill is pointed. (Australian Gannets have a shorter throat stripe.) The dark immature is spotted with white, but is larger than similar birds. Found in coastal waters, seldom over the open ocean. Congregates over shoals of fish, diving into the water. Breeds in colonies on islands.
(Witmalgas)

53

Nbr

Swift Tern

The yellow bill distinguishes it from all other terns, even those with orange bills. Slightly smaller than the Caspian Tern. The black cap extends only to above the eye; the forehead is white. The cap of the non-breeding bird is greyer. The tail is deeply forked. Found on estuaries and at river mouths, often in association with other terns and gulls. Breeds in colonies on islands or vleis near the coast.
(Geelbekseeswael)

324

Nbr

Br

Common Tern

One of the most common coastal terns during summer. The non-breeding bird has a black bill, but the forehead is white. (The bill and legs of the very similar Arctic Tern are shorter. The Antarctic Tern has grey underparts.) The breeding bird, which is seldom seen, has a red bill tipped with black. Usually mixes with other terns. Dives into the water for food.
(Gewone seeswael)

327

North. hemisph.

Caspian Tern

The largest tern in the region. Its large size and the massive red bill distinguish it from other similar terns. (The Swift Tern has a yellow bill.) The cap of the non-breeding bird is dark grey. Found on estuaries and large inland waters. The flight is slow, like that of a gull. When foraging, it hovers with the bill pointed downwards and then dives into the water to catch fish.
(Reuseseeswael)

322

Whiskered Tern

This tern and the White-winged Tern occur mostly on inland waters. Both have square tails, unlike other terns. In the breeding plumage the Whiskered Tern is unmistakable. Non-breeding birds resemble non-breeding White-winged Terns, but are usually seen in winter when the latter are absent. Small flocks fly low over the water, quartering to and fro. The nest floats on the water.
(Witbaardmeerswael)

338

White-winged Tern

The most common inland tern during summer. The non-breeding plumage is grey and white, with dark patches behind the eyes and on the crown. (The non-breeding Whiskered Tern is very similar, but is seen during autumn and winter.) Before it leaves for the Northern Hemisphere in April, the pied breeding plumage may be seen. Large flocks forage over freshwater.
(Witvlerkmeerswael)

339

Eurasia

11

Group 2: Swimming and diving waterbirds

Waterbirds which swim or dive from the surface of the water may occur on either marine or inland waters. These include the **penguins, pelicans, cormorants, darters, ducks, geese, grebes, moorhens** and **coots**. All have webbed toes, except grebes, moorhens and coots whose toes are lobed.

Cormorants and **darters** are mostly dark in colour. They swim very low in the water, diving for their food. After swimming they have to dry their non-waterproof feathers by sunning themselves with outstretched wings.

Penguins are well-known ocean birds. **Pelicans** are huge white birds characterized by the enormous pouch below the bill used to catch fish.

Ducks and **geese** have flattened bills. Many ducks filter fine food particles from the water, while the geese are more adapted to feed on grass and leaves.

Grebes, moorhens and **coots** are often mistaken for ducks, but have pointed bills. Grebes feed by diving for small animals, while the moorhens and coots are more vegetarian.

Imm

Ad Br

African Darter
The long thin neck, slender body and straight pointed bill distinguish it from the cormorants. Immature and non-breeding birds have pale, not black, underparts. Occurs on most inland waters. Swims with the body submerged, only part of the neck and head visible. Like the cormorants, it dries its outspread wings in the sun after swimming. Breeds in colonies.
(Afrikaanse slanghalsvoël)

60

4

Ad Br

Imm

White-breasted Cormorant
The largest cormorant in the region. The white throat and breast and the heavy bill are characteristic. Immatures have white bellies. (The immature Reed Cormorant is smaller and its belly is off-white.) The breeding bird may have a white spot on the thigh. Found along the coast and on larger inland waters. Often perches on dead trees and flies low over the water.
(Witborsduiker)

55

3

Cape Cormorant

The adult is green-black with a yellow patch at the base of the bill. The eyes are green. Non-breeding birds and immatures are dark brown with paler bellies. (The Crowned Cormorant is smaller, has a crest and red eyes.) The most common cormorant along our coast. Forages in large flocks and often flies in long lines. Roosts and breeds in colonies on guano islands. (Trekduiker)

56

Bank Cormorant

A black, robust cormorant with a crested head and sometimes a white rump. (The Crowned Cormorant is smaller and the Cape Cormorant has a yellow throat, but no crest.) Prefers the colder water along the west coast and is always found near the coast. Forages either alone or in small flocks. Roosts and breeds on coastal islands or on isolated rocky outcrops on the mainland. (Bankduiker)

57

Reed Cormorant

A small cormorant with a long tail and red eyes. When breeding it is darker, especially on the belly, and has a crest on the head. The immature has off-white underparts. Occurs widely on inland waters. (The similar Crowned Cormorant is a marine bird along the west coast.) Swims low in the water. Like all cormorants it often sits with outspread wings in the sun. Breeds in colonies with other waterbirds. (Rietduiker)

58

Imm

Ad Br

Jackass Penguin

The only penguin to breed along this coast. The upright stance distinguishes it on land. When swimming only the head is visible and the white crescent on the side of the head is conspicuous. The head and back of the immature are dark grey and the underparts a dull white. Forages at sea but roosts on land. Breeds in colonies on islands along the coast.
(Brilpikkewyn)

3

Eastern White Pelican

The larger of the two pelicans. The white colour, pink facial skin and yellow pouch distinguish it from the Pink-backed Pelican. The underwing is black and white in flight. The immature has brown wings and a pale yellow breast. Found along the coast and on larger inland waters. May associate with the Pink-backed Pelican. Flocks often chase fish into shallow water before scooping them up.
(Oostelike witpelikaan)

49

Pink-backed Pelican

The greyer plumage distinguishes it from the Eastern White Pelican. It is also smaller, has a yellow bill and a grey or pink pouch. The underwing is uniformly coloured in flight. The immature is brown, but not as brown as the immature Eastern White Pelican. Found on estuaries, river mouths and larger inland waters. Associates with the White Pelican. Forages alone, but breeds in colonies.
(Kleinpelikaan)

50

White-faced Duck

The upright stance, black head and neck, and the white face are characteristic. (The head of the female SA Shelduck is grey at the back.) The immature has a pale brown (not white) face. Its call consists of three whistles. Found on rivers and large inland waters with sufficient vegetation. Swims with the neck extended and dives regularly. Forages also at night. Breeds in family groups.

(Nonnetjie-eend)

99

Imm

Ad

Fulvous Duck

The head and body are golden brown, the bill and legs grey. The creamy-white feathers on the flanks are characteristic. The call is two consecutive whistles. Found on large, quiet inland waters with sufficient surface vegetation. Dives frequently for food. Mixes sometimes with White-faced-Ducks. Spends much time on the water's edge, but remains shy and wary.

(Fluiteend)

100

Yellow-billed Duck

A grey-brown duck with a characteristic yellow bill. Each feather has a lighter edge, giving a scaled appearance. The green secondaries are conspicuous in flight. (The African Black Duck has a dark bill and yellow legs.) Is widely distributed on inland waters. Flies high and fast, but does not dive often. Groups linger along the edge of the water.

(Geelbekeend)

104

15

Egyptian Goose

A brown goose with darker upperparts and red legs. There is a dark brown patch around the eyes and a brown patch on the breast, hence the Afrikaans name. In flight the wings are characteristically white with black tips. Occurs on most inland waters and estuaries. Roosts near water. Females are noisy, while males hiss.
Breeds in a variety of sites even on buildings far away from water.
(Kolgans)

102

South African Shelduck

Chestnut brown with dark legs and a grey head. The female's face is white. (The White-faced Duck is darker and the back of the head is black.) Resembles the Egyptian Goose in flight, but is more coppery. Found on most inland waters, but prefers brackish pans. Often lingers along the water's edge. Females court the males. Breeds in winter. Nests in aardvark or other holes.
(Kopereend)

103

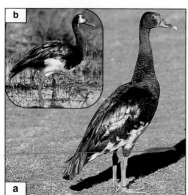

Spur-winged Goose

The largest of our waterfowl. The belly is white, the rest of the plumage is black with a glossy green shine, but colour variations occur (a and b). The legs and bill are pinkish red. Males are larger than females and have a growth on the forehead. Flocks occur on most larger inland waters surrounded by grasslands. Breeds in pairs on smaller bodies of water. Shy and wary. Often perches on dead trees or near the water's edge.   (Wildemakou)

116

16

African Black Duck

The upperparts are dark brown, spotted with white. The rest of the body is grey-brown, the bill is dark and the legs yellow. (Yellow-billed Ducks have yellow bills and dark legs.) The green secondaries are conspicuous in flight. Found in territorial pairs on shallow rivers in wooded areas. Very shy; takes off at the last moment when disturbed. Flies low and very fast over the water.

(Afrikaanse swarteend)

105

 6

Cape Shoveller

The broad, dark bill of this pale brown duck is characteristic. The legs are yellow, but orange when breeding. In flight the wing has a blue leading edge. This is separated from the green secondaries by a white band. The eyes of the males are yellow, females have dark eyes. Prefers shallow temporary pools. Takes off steeply and flies fast. Often lingers at the water's edge.

(Kaapse slopeend)

112

 9

Southern Pochard

The male has a dark brown head, neck and back. The belly is light brown. The eye is a conspicuous red. The female is paler with dark eyes. A white crescent stretches from behind the eyes to the side of the neck. Both sexes have blue-grey bills. (Maccoa Duck males have blue bills. Females and non-breeding males have pale lines below the eyes.) Prefers deep, clean inland water. Shy.

(Bruineend)

113

 9

Cape Teal

A pale, small duck with darker spots and a pink bill. (The Red-billed Teal has a red bill and a dark cap with white cheeks.) The wings appear dark in flight. The secondaries are white with a central green triangle. Prefers shallow inland brackish water like salt pans and marshes, but also estuaries and tidal flats. Often rises to circle and land nearby. Dives when foraging for food.
(Teeleend)

106

Red-billed Teal

Could be confused with the Cape Teal, but the head has a dark cap and white cheeks. The bill is characteristically red, not pink. The pale secondaries are visible in flight. (The Hottentot Teal is smaller and buffier, with a blue-grey bill.) Found on most inland waters. Seen mostly in flocks, especially at the end of winter. Occurs in pairs when breeding.
(Rooibekeend)

108

Hottentot Teal

A very small duck. Could be confused with the Red-billed Teal, but the bill is blue-grey, not red, and the head pattern is slightly different. The overall appearance is yellow-ish-brown. Shows green secondaries in flight. Pairs and small flocks prefer quiet inland waters with some vegetation where they are well camouflaged. Often rests on the water's edge.
(Gevlekte eend)

107

Pygmy Goose

Our smallest duck. The underparts are orange, the upperparts dark green and the face white. The short bill is yellow. The male has a large green patch on the side of the neck, which is absent in females and immatures. The white secondaries are clearly visible in flight. Prefers clear inland waters covered with vegetation where it is easily overlooked. Spends most of its time on the water.
(Dwerggans)   114

  9

Knob-billed Duck

The upperwings are metallic blue with a glossy sheen, the underwings are black. The underparts are white. Males are bigger than females, and have a fleshy growth on the bill. This gets larger when breeding. Found on marshes, floodplains and shallow pans with surface vegetation in bushveld areas. Perches in trees or on the ground close to water. Males often have more than one female.
(Knobbeleend)   115

 8

Red-knobbed Coot

A pitch-black waterbird with a characteristic white bill and frontal shield. The eyes and the two knobs on the forehead (hence the name) are red. These knobs are swollen in breeding birds. The grey legs are greenish when breeding. (The Common Moorhen has a red bill and frontal shield.) Found in large numbers on most inland waters. Often chase each other while swimming.
(Bleshoender)

228

 5

19

Imm
Ad

Common Moorhen

The yellow legs, red frontal shield and bill with a yellow tip are characteristic. Except for the white undertail and the white feathers on the flanks, the plumage is black. (The rarer Lesser Moorhen is smaller, the bill mostly yellow and the legs pale green.) Inhabits reed beds and sedges around most bodies of water. Swims most of the time, also climbs over reeds or walks around in the shallows. (Grootwaterhoender)

226

7

Nbr
Br

Dabchick

Smallest of the three grebes – smaller than any duck. When breeding the throat and sides of the neck are rufous and there is a white spot at the base of the bill. The dark eyes and pale (not white) underparts distinguish it from the Black-necked Grebe. Found commonly on most permanent inland waters with vegetation. Dives frequently. Breeds throughout the year. (Kleindobbertjie)

8

3

Great Crested Grebe

The largest grebe in the region. The white crest, dark cap and dark red eyes are characteristic. Breeding birds may be confused with the Black-necked Grebe which is smaller and lacks the crest. Found on larger bodies of water with sedges and other emergent vegetation. Sometimes ventures onto the sea. Dives for food. Has an elaborate courtship display. (Kuifkopdobbertjie)

6

3

Group 3: Larger wading birds

The larger wading birds are characterized by their long legs. The majority are associated with water areas, although some species are often found in other moist habitats. These are the **herons, egrets, storks, cranes, Hamerkop, ibises, spoonbills** and **flamingos**.

Herons and **egrets** fly with their heads tucked into their shoulders. Their bills are long and slender. **Storks** are voiceless, but clap their heavy bills. **Cranes** have far-carrying trumpeting calls heard during their elaborate courtship dances. The long decurved bills of **ibises** probe for small animals hidden in mud or soil. The unique bill of **flamingos** is used to filter plankton from the water. No other birds can be confused with the **Hamerkop** and **African Spoonbill**.

Bustards, korhaans and the **Ostrich** are, strictly speaking, not wading birds as they do not have the habit of wading in shallow water. Most bustards and korhaans occur in dry open habitats, but some inhabit wooded areas.

Grey Heron

The bill and legs are yellowish. The crown is white with a black band just above the eye. The front of the white neck has black streaks. In flight the underwing is grey. Young birds are similar to, but much duller than adults and could be mistaken for the young Black-headed Heron. Frequents shallow water, quietly waiting for prey. Breeds in colonies with other herons and cormorants.
(Bloureier)

62

Black-headed Heron

The top of the head and back of the neck are black, the bill and legs dark. In flight the black flight feathers distinguish it from the Grey Heron. Young birds are similar to young Grey Herons, but the dark cap of the head extends to below the eye. Found in marshes, shallows and open patches of grass away from water. Roosts and breeds in colonies in trees and on islands.
(Swartkopreier)

63

Imm

Ad

21

Goliath Heron

Our largest heron. The back and wings are dark grey with a rufous neck and underparts. The bill is very large and the long legs hang slightly below the horizontal in flight. Young birds are browner above and buff underneath. Could at a distance be mistaken for the Purple Heron, which is smaller, more slenderly built and with streaks down the side of the neck. Stands for long periods in deeper water, waiting for prey. (Reusereier)

64

Purple Heron

A slender heron with a long thin neck and a slender, yellowish bill. The back is grey-brown and the neck orange-brown, streaked black on the sides. The crown of the head is black, but the throat is white. At a distance it is similar to the Goliath Heron, but much smaller, more slender and without a rufous crown. A shy heron which hides among the reeds of quiet dams and marshes. Roosts in colonies. (Rooireier)

65

Common Squacco Heron

The breast is white, and the back and neck light brown, streaked on the neck. The legs and bill are yellowish. Breeding birds have blue bills tipped with black, and red legs; the back is then rufous-brown and the crown dark. The brilliant white wings are conspicuous in flight. A very shy bird. Frequents quiet waters with plenty of shelter where it hides quietly. Roosts in colonies.
(Gewone ralreier)

72

Great White Egret

The largest of the white egrets. The neck and legs are very long. The bill is usually yellow, but black at the start of the breeding season. A dark line extends from the bill to under and behind the eye. (This distinguishes it from the Yellow-billed Egret which is smaller and has yellow upper legs.) Prefers shallow inland waters where it stands motionless in wait for prey.
(Grootwitreier)

Nbr

Br

66

3

Little Egret

The slender black bill, black legs and yellow toes distinguish it from other white egrets. The long head plumes are present throughout the year, but the breast and back plumes during the breeding season only. It is larger but more slender than the Cattle Egret. Feeds in shallow inland waters and visits intertidal pools, usually disturbing prey with its yellow toes. Roosts and breeds in colonies, but hunts alone.
(Kleinwitreier)

67

3

Cattle Egret

Adults have yellow bills and legs (orange-red at the beginning of the breeding season). Orange plumes are present on the head, breast and back when breeding. Immatures have dark bills and legs like the Little Egret; however, their necks are shorter and the toes dark. Forages in flocks alongside larger herbivores like cattle to catch insects. Flies in "V" formation to roosting trees near water.
(Veereier/Bosluisvoël)

Br

Nbr

71

3

Black Egret

It is dark grey, but looks black at a distance. The bill is black. The head carries a long crest. The yellow toes are orange-red at the beginning of the breeding season. (The similar Slaty Egret of the Okavango has yellow eyes and legs, and a rufous throat.) Inhabits shallow inland waters and estuaries. Brings its wings forward to form a characteristic umbrella-like canopy when fishing (b). Groups sometimes fish co-operatively.   (Swartreier)

69

Black-crowned Night Heron

The black crown and back, grey wings and red eyes are characteristic. The yellow legs become reddish during courtship. Breeding birds have three long white plumes on the crown. Immatures are brown, spotted on the back and streaked on the underparts. The eyes are orange. (The similar Bittern is larger and clearly streaked.) Prefers quiet, densely vegetated waters. Nocturnal. Hides in trees or among plants during the day.   (Gewone nagreier)

76

Green-backed Heron

The yellow legs (reddish when breeding) and grey-green back with white-edged feathers on the wing are characteristic. The crown is black with black plumes. A black line extends from the crown to underneath the eye. The head is usually tucked into the shoulders. Immatures have streaked breasts and dark brown backs and their wings are spotted white. Prefers dense vegetation near water. Breeds low down in trees.   (Groenrugreier)

74

Greater Flamingo

A large white bird with very long legs. The white plumage of this bird has a slight pink sheen. The pink bill is tipped black. In flight the deep red wing patches can be seen. (Lesser Flamingoes are much pinker and have darker bills.) Immatures are grey. Found in large shallow-water areas, often marine or saline water. Forages with the bill held upside down in the water. Breeds in colonies on saline pans. (Grootflamink)

96

Lesser Flamingo

Differs from the Greater Flamingo in its smaller size, stronger pink colour and dark red bill, tipped black. Immatures are grey. Found on large shallow-water areas, especially marine or saline water. Also feeds on plankton, but forages in the top layers of the water while the Greater Flamingo stirs plankton from the muddy substrate. Breeds in colonies on mud flats in saline pans. (Kleinflamink)

97

Ad

Imm

Marabou Stork

A large stork with a very large, grey-brown bill. The dirty-pink head and neck are bare. The underparts are white and the back and wings dark grey. The dark wings are also clearly visible in light. Immatures have a crown of white down. Forages at carcasses or at rubbish dumps, often in association with vultures. Stands resting for long periods. In contrast with other storks, it flies with the head tucked into the shoulders. (Maraboe)

89

Woolly-necked Stork

The dark brown back and wings, and white woolly head and neck are characteristic. The face is black and at the base of the bill is a white patch. In flight the white undertail coverts extend beyond the dark tail. Immatures lack the glossy sheen on the back. Found at shallow water, but prefers swampy wooded regions. Walks slowly, often standing quietly for long periods in wait for prey.
(Wolnekooievaar)

86

African Open-billed Stork

The plumage is very dark brown, the legs are black. The feathers on the shoulders, neck and breast show a slight glossy green. The large, yellow-brown bill has a large gap between upper and lower jaw. Immatures lack the gap in the bill. Found at larger inland waters in wooded areas. Often stands quietly or searches for snails and mussels in shallow water. Breeds in colonies in trees.
(Afrikaanse oopbekooievaar)

87

Saddle-billed Stork

A very large black and white stork with long legs and neck. The enormous bill is banded red and black, with a yellow saddle on top of the base. Females have yellow eyes. Males have black eyes and small yellow wattles on the chin. Immatures are greyer with a dark brown bill. Frequents shallow inland waters and rivers. Shy and wary. Roosts and breeds in trees close to water.
(Saalbekooievaar)

88

26

Yellow-billed Stork

The yellow bill, slightly decurved at the tip, and bare red face are characteristic. The white plumage (especially on the back) is slightly pinkish when breeding. The flight feathers and the tail are black. (White Storks have red bills and white tails.) Immatures are brown with orange faces. Found at larger water areas especially in wooded regions. Will stand quietly for long periods in shallow water.
(Nimmersat)

90

Ad

Imm

3

White Stork

The plumage is mostly white, apart from the black flight feathers. The legs and pointed bill are red. (Yellow-billed Storks have yellow bills curving down at the tip, bare red faces and black tails.) Forages on grasslands and farmlands, where it often mixes with Abdim's Stork. Flocks often circle high up in the sky in search of food. Roosts and breeds in colonies in trees.
(Witooievaar)

83

3

Abdim's Stork

The deep red knees and toes contrast with the dirty-pink of the rest of the legs. The bill is horn-coloured and the cheeks are blue. The body is black with a white rump. (The rarer Black Stork is larger and has a red bill, cheeks and legs.) Forages on grassland and farmlands. Large flocks often circle high up in the air, or walk slowly over open veld in search of food.
(Kleinswartooievaar)

85

North Africa

27

Hamerkop

The strong black bill and the crested head led to its name, meaning 'hammerhead'. The plumage is brown. Found widely on inland waters, estuaries and even temporary pools. Forages in shallow water by shuffling its feet, thus disturbing small animals, especially Clawed Toads (Platannas). Its nest is an enormous structure of sticks and grasses: up to 2 m in diameter, built in a tree or on a rock.
(Hamerkop)

81

Unique
3

African Spoonbill

The bare red face and legs, and flat spoon-shaped bill characterize this brilliant white bird. The bill is grey on top, edged red. Immatures have black legs, dull yellow bills and black-streaked heads. Found on shallow inland waters. When foraging, it walks slowly while swinging its bill from side to side. Roosts and breeds in colonies, mostly in trees.
(Afrikaanse lepelaar)

95

3

Sacred Ibis

A white ibis with a bare black head, neck and legs. The black bill is conspicuously long and decurved. Long black plumes grow on the rump. The necks of immatures are spotted with white. Found at inland waters, grasslands and estuaries. Feeds mostly on insects, but the diet is varied and includes carrion. Flocks fly in a "V" formation from and to the colonies. Roosts and breeds in colonies in trees.
(Skoorsteenveër)

91

2

Glossy Ibis

A smallish, slender ibis. The plumage is glossy brown with a green sheen on the back and wings. (The Hadeda Ibis is more robustly built.) The heads and necks of non-breeding birds are spotted white. Immatures resemble non-breeding birds, but are darker. Prefers shallow flooded areas in grasslands, such as marshes, floodplains and sewage works. Roosts and breeds in colonies. (Glansibis)

93

Br

Nbr

Hadeda Ibis

A grey-brown, stockily built ibis. On the shoulder is an iridescent pink patch. The rest of the wing has a green sheen. The bill has a red upper edge. (Larger and more robustly built than the Glossy Ibis.) The call is a loud "haaaa" or "ha-ha-hadeda". Frequents grassy areas, such as sports grounds, parks and landing strips, often near water. Small flocks roost in trees. Breeds in pairs in large trees, even in gardens. (Hadeda)

94

Southern Bald Ibis

The long bill, bare crown and legs are red. The rest of the face and throat is creamy white. The plumage is glossy green with a coppery patch on the shoulders, but appears black at a distance. The heads and necks of immatures are covered with grey down. Found in montane grasslands, especially burnt areas, but also in farmlands. Roosts and breeds in colonies on cliffs. (Suidelike kalkoenibis)

92

Kori Bustard

The largest bustard in the region and our heaviest flying bird. The grey neck and the crested head distinguish it from the other two large bustards: Stanley's and Ludwig's Bustards. The back and wings are pale brown. Found in open grassy areas. Holds the bill slightly upwards when walking. Does not fly often. Males are larger than females and have an elaborate courtship display. Breeds on the ground.
(Gompou)

230

Red-crested Korhaan

Pale "V" marks on the back and wings are characteristic. The belly is black with two white patches on the upper breast of the male and a white band in the female. Females have brown heads, males blue-grey necks and heads. Found in bushveld and wooded areas. During courtship the male flies vertically into the air and tumbles down to the ground. Its red crest can then sometimes be seen.
(Boskorhaan)

237

Black-bellied Korhaan

The black triangles on the back and the long yellowish legs are characteristic. The black belly of the male extends into a thin line on the neck to the throat. (The Red-crested Korhaan has shorter legs and neck, and pale "V" marks on the back.) Females have white bellies. When displaying during courtship the male flies a distance and glides downwards with his wings held in a "V". Breeds on the ground.
(Langbeenkorhaan)

238

30

Blue Korhaan

The blue-grey neck and underparts are characteristic. The back is brown and the legs are yellow. The sides of the head are white. The female resembles the male but has a brown patch on the cheeks. At a distance it could be confused with the male Black or White-quilled Korhaan. Found on grasslands, farmlands and Karoo-like scrub. Breeds on the ground. Will chase even large animals from its nest. (Bloukorhaan)

234

White-quilled Korhaan

The banded back distinguishes both sexes from other korhaans, except the similar Black Korhaan which occurs in the Cape fynbos region. The legs are yellow and the bill mainly red. The male's black head and neck, and white ear patches are characteristic. In flight the white wing patches distinguish it from the Black Korhaan. Males often stand on a raised perch or circle noisily. (Witvlerkkorhaan)

239b

Karoo Korhaan

A brown korhaan with yellowish legs. The black patch on the chin is characteristic. (The similar, but more boldly marked Rüppell's Korhaan occurs further northwards in the Namib desert.) Prefers stony areas with patches of bushes and grass. Easily overlooked. Drinks regularly in the morning and late afternoon. Crouches down when disturbed, rather than running away. Breeds on the ground. (Vaalkorhaan)

235

Blue Crane

A large blue-grey bird with a long neck and black legs. The bill is pink-brown and the head very large. The long "tail" is really the inner flight feathers hanging over the tail. The call is a loud trumpeting. Found on farmlands and on the edges of marshes in grasslands. Flocks are nomadic when not breeding. During the breeding season pairs or family groups are seen.
(Bloukraanvoël)

208

Southern Crowned Crane

A very attractive bird. The spiny yellow crest resembles a pincushion. The body is mostly grey with white patches on the wing. The head is black with white cheeks. The call is "ma-hem", hence the Afrikaans name. The habitat is marshes, farmlands and moist grassland. Pairs and groups often dance in display. Non-breeding groups are nomadic. In pairs when breeding.
(Mahem)

209

Ostrich

Unmistakable. Very large flightless birds with bare necks and legs. Females are grey-brown, males are black with dirty-white flight and tail feathers. Breeding males have red shins. Hybrids of the North and South African races are kept on farms. Can run very fast, up to 60 km/h. Males often keep more than one female; these lay their eggs in a single nest; only the senior hen incubates.
(Volstruis)

1

Group 4: Smaller waders

The smaller waders are long-legged birds, smaller than a guineafowl. Most, although certainly not all, are associated with water, often feeding in the shallows.

Dikkops are nocturnal birds as indicated by their large eyes. Only the Water Dikkop occurs near water. **Coursers** are birds of open country, mostly occurring in arid areas where they are easily overlooked.

Crakes, gallinules and **jacanas** are not typical waders. They are more robustly built and have relatively shorter legs with very long toes. These aid them in moving over floating vegetation.

Plovers and **sandpipers** are very similar in body size and shape. Plovers, however, have fairly short bills. All sandpipers and their close relatives (except the Ethiopian Snipe) are migrant visitors from the north, seen here mostly in their non-breeding plumage. The **oystercatchers** are boldly coloured shorebirds. **Avocets** and **stilts** are characterized by their extremely long, thin bills and legs.

Spotted Dikkop

A plover-like bird with large yellow eyes and long yellow legs. The upperparts and wings have bold dark brown spots. (Water Dikkops are streaked on the back.) Although widely distributed, it prefers open patches with short grass. Secretive during the day, but active during the night. Its loud piping call is often heard at night or after rains. Non-breeding birds gather in flocks.

(Dikkop)

297

Water Dikkop

Resembles the Spotted Dikkop, but has a conspicuous grey wingbar. The upperparts are streaked, not spotted. Found mainly along inland waters, but sometimes on beaches along the coast. Although also a nocturnal bird, it is more often seen during the day than the Spotted Dikkop. Walks slowly while foraging. Runs off when disturbed, but can fly strongly.

(Waterdikkop)

298

Burchell's Courser

Similar to Temminck's Courser, but the back of the crown is a characteristic blue-grey and the belly is white. Shows a white area on the wing in flight. Easily overlooked. Most common on the open plains of Namibia. Sways its body and bobs the tail when alarmed. Runs very fast, stopping suddenly to peck at food or to hide behind some shelter. Nests on the ground.
(Bloukopdrawwertjie)

299

  ₂ **None**

Temminck's Courser

Similar to Burchell's Courser in appearance and habits. The entire crown is rufous-brown. The upper belly is rufous, not white. In flight shows no white on the wing. Easily overlooked. Found in open areas with short or no grass, often congregating on burnt veld. When alarmed, it moves the body up and down by flexing its legs. Nests on the ground.
(Trekdrawwertjie)

300

  ₂ **None**

Double-banded Courser

A pale courser with mottled upperparts and a speckled head. The two black bands across the breast, forming rings around the neck, are diagnostic. The legs are white. The immature is a duller version of the adult. Prefers dry barren flats where it is easily overlooked. Shy and wary. Bobs its head to and fro when alarmed. Runs quickly to peck at food. Active day and night. Nests on the ground.
(Dubbelbanddrawwertjie)

301

 ₁ **None**

Black Crake

A black bird, except for the red eyes and legs, and the yellow bill. The immature is olive-brown. Found on well-vegetated inland waters. Not as shy as other crakes and thus often seen in the open, especially after rains. Flicks its tail and walks with jerking movements. Sometimes swims. The call is a characteristic "k-k-k-krrung", repeated several times.
(Swartriethaan)

213

Purple Gallinule

The body is a deep blue, but greenish on the wings and back. The red legs, bill and frontal shield are characteristic. (The rarer, shyer Lesser Gallinule has a blue frontal shield.) Immatures are brownish. Occurs in the tall swampy vegetation around inland waters. Shy and secretive, but sometimes comes into the open to forage. Often holds food with one foot.
(Grootkoningriethaan)

223

African Jacana

The extremely long toes and the rich chestnut plumage characterize this bird. The bill and frontal shield are blue. Immatures (not to be confused with the smaller Lesser Jacana) are duller with a black eyestripe and white eyebrow. The long toes support it over floating vegetation. Often turns over leaves to look for food. One female mates with a number of males during the season, but each male incubates the eggs and raises his own chicks. (Grootlangtoon)

240

Three-banded Plover

A very common small plover. Identified by its two black breastbands separated by a white bar which extends around the neck. The yellow eye has a red ring. The bill is red with a black tip. Well camouflaged in spite of the bright colours. Found commonly on the shorelines of inland waters, less often on the seashore. Runs with jerky movements. Nests on exposed flats.
(Driebandstrandkiewiet)

249

Chestnut-banded Plover

A very small plover. The narrow chestnut breastband is characteristic, but is paler in females, and greyer and incomplete in immatures. The male has a black band from the ears across the crown. Prefers saline or brackish water, especially along the coast, but also inland. The pale colour camouflages it well in this habitat. May forage with other small waders.
(Rooibandstrandkiewiet)

247

Kittlitz's Plover

The yellow-brown breast and the black head pattern are characteristic. Has longer legs than other small plovers. Immatures have a faint brownish pattern on the head. Prefers extensive shores of inland waters, but is also found on dry pans and areas with short grass. Easily overlooked. Runs and flies fast. Usually nests in a deep scrape in the ground.
(Geelborsstrandkiewiet)

248

White-fronted Plover

A small plover with a white belly and a white back collar (the northern race, b, being yellowish). A dark line connects the bill and eye, the forehead is white. The male has a darker forecrown than the female. This is the most common small plover on the seashore and along some larger inland waters. Runs very fast while searching for food, with the head tucked into the shoulders. Flight swift and low.
(Vaalstrandkiewiet)

246

Grey Plover

A medium-sized, robustly built plover. The greyish upperparts are mottled with white. Diagnostic are the black "armpits" which are shown in flight. (The Red Knot's bill is longer and its legs are shorter.) In spring and autumn it might be seen in partial or full breeding plumage with a black face and underparts. Prefers coastal flats, but might be seen at larger inland waters. Shy and wary.
(Grysstrandkiewiet)

254

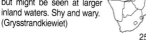

Eurasia

Ruddy Turnstone

The short bill, long body shape and shortish, orange legs are characteristic. In the breeding plumage, which is sometimes seen at the end of the summer, the bird has a bolder head and neck pattern and is more distinctly rufous on the back. Prefers rocky coastal shores. Turns over stones, shells and other objects when foraging. When disturbed, it flies off low while calling.
(Rooisteenloper)

262

North. hemisph.

37

Crowned Plover

The black and white ring around the black cap, together with the red legs and bill makes this plover unmistakable. Immatures are browner versions of adults. Found on areas with short grass, often on lawns. Very alert and noisy, especially when breeding. Dive-bombs enemies or tries to lure them away from the nest with a "broken wing" display.
(Kroonkiewiet)

255

Black-winged Plover

Could only be confused with the Lesser Black-winged Plover which occurs in the north-east. The Black-winged Plover is characterized by the white forehead touching the eye, yellow eye with a red ring, and reddish legs. Prefers areas with short or burnt grass. Similar in habits to the Crowned Plover in whose company it is often seen. Easily overlooked.
(Grootswartvlerkkiewiet)

257

Blacksmith Plover

A characteristic, boldly marked black and white plover with grey wings and back. Immatures are brown, but show the same general patterning as adults. The name refers to its call, sounding like a blacksmith's hammer striking an anvil. Usually silent, but calls loudly when alarmed. Found near water. Sometimes stirs up small prey with its feet.
(Bontkiewiet)

258

Wattled Plover

The largest plover in the region. The yellow wattles, bill and legs, and the white forehead are diagnostic. The body is mostly brown. (The White-crowned Plover has larger wattles, white underparts and occurs on the sandbanks of the larger rivers in the north-east only.) Prefers moist grasslands near water. Unlike other plovers it often nests in small open patches among taller stands of grass. (Lelkiewiet) 260

Whimbrel

A largish wader with a decurved bill. The crown is dark brown with a pale central stripe. (The rarer Eurasian Curlew is larger, lighter in colour and lacks the head pattern.) In flight shows a large white rump. Occurs widely on marine shores, but seldom on inland waters. Moves with a jerky gait, while probing for worms and other invertebrates in the soft substrate. The flight is fast and straight. (Kleinwulp) 290

North. hemisph.

Ethiopian Snipe

The very long bill, but relatively short legs are diagnostic. The back is striped golden. (The rare Great Snipe has more heavily marked buff underparts.) Found widely in shallow water, preferably close to plant cover where it hides when disturbed. Zigzags low when flushed. A "drumming" sound is produced with its tail feathers during the diving display flight. Often active at night. (Afrikaanse snip) 286

Common Sandpiper

A smallish sandpiper which bobs its tail frequently. Diagnostic is the white area around the shoulders. The back appears to be plain dark brown. (The Green Sandpiper is bigger with a more prominent eyebrow.) Flies low, with a spasmodic wing action. Frequents most shorelines, inland and marine. Does not form flocks and is thus easily overlooked. The only visiting wader that often roosts with resident birds. (Gewone ruiter)

264

Eurasia

Wood Sandpiper

The spotted upperparts and the broad, pale eyebrow are characteristic. The yellow-green legs are long, but the bill is relatively short. In flight shows a clear white rump and underwing coverts, and a barred tail. (The Green Sandpiper's back is darker.) Found mostly at inland waters, preferring those with a marshy shore. When flushed, it flies low at first, but then rises. Bobs its body when settling. (Bosruiter)

266

Eurasia

Ruff/Reeve

The scaled colour pattern on the back and wings is diagnostic. The blunt-tipped bill is very slightly decurved. At the base of the bill is a white patch. The female, known as a Reeve, is much smaller than the male. The leg colour varies between individuals. Prefers the shallows of inland waters, but is also found in flooded grass-lands and even on the coast. Forms huge flocks, often with other sandpipers. (Kemphaan)

284

Eurasia

Marsh Sandpiper

Easily confused with the Common Greenshank, but is a smaller, more slenderly built bird with a straight thin bill and longer legs. In flight also resembles the Common Greenshank with an extensive white rump. Frequents inland shallows, where it is a fairly tame bird. Usually solitary. Forages with quick and active movements, often sweeping the bill from side to side.
(Moerasruiter)

269

Eurasia

Common Greenshank

Resembles the Marsh Sandpiper, but is larger and more robust. The bill is long and stout, slightly upcurved and grey at the base. A dark line extends from the bill to the eye. Calls loudly when flushed. Found at inland waters and coastal areas. Often seen in the company of the Marsh Sandpiper, but is shy and wary. Often enters deeper water while feeding.
(Gewone groenpootruiter)

270

Eurasia

Curlew Sandpiper

A very common small wader, characterized by a decurved bill and a uniformly coloured back. The head is normally tucked into the shoulders, giving it a hunched appearance. Shows a broad white rump in flight. The underparts are a rich chestnut in the breeding plumage which is sometimes seen. Found on both inland and marine shores, often in large numbers with other waders.
(Krombekstrandloper)

272

 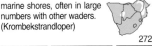

Asia

41

Red Knot

A small, but chunkily built wader with short legs. The bill is heavy, straight or slightly decurved; the legs are relatively short. (The Curlew Sandpiper is smaller with a more decurved bill.) At the end of summer it may moult into the breeding plumage with chestnut underparts. Occurs in dense flocks on areas exposed by the tide, especially along the west coast. The flock's flight is fast and highly synchronized.
(Rooiknoet)

271

Asia

Little Stint

The smallest of the more common waders in southern Africa. The blotched upperparts are greyish-brown, but more rufous in the breeding plumage. (Although the bill is relatively short, that of the rare Red-necked Stint is even shorter.) Prefers the muddy shores or shallows of inland waters, but is also found in coastal areas. Very active. The flocks are sometimes very large, also including other wader species.　　(Kleinstrandloper)

274

Eurasia

Sanderling

A small, very pale wader. The black shoulder patches are conspicuous. In flight it shows a broad white wingbar and a dark central line on the rump. In the breeding plumage the upperparts, head, neck and breast are a light chestnut. Common on sandy beaches, where flocks run up and down following the waves. This characteristic behaviour is quick and very active. Flies fast.
(Drietoonstrandloper)

281

North. hemisph

African Black Oystercatcher

Easily recognized by its black plumage, together with the red legs, bill and eyes. (The rare European Oystercatcher has a white belly.) The immature is browner. Prefers rocky and sandy coasts. Limpets are levered off the rocks, and snail shells are smashed or opened with the powerful bill. When disturbed the flock flies off, calling together.
(Afrikaanse swarttobie)

244

Pied Avocet

Characterized by its black and white plumage and its long, thin, upcurved bill. (The Black-winged Stilt has long red legs and a straight bill.) The immature is dark brown and white. Prefers shallow water, where it forages by sweeping its bill from side to side. Sometimes swims. Non-breeding birds often gather in very large flocks, moving from one suitable feeding site to the next.
(Bontelsie)

294

Black-winged Stilt

This black and white bird is characterized by its long slender bill and the disproportionately long red legs. (The Avocet has grey legs and a thin upcurved bill.) The crown may be black. Immatures are grey on the head and nape. The call is like a plover's. Prefers inland waters. Forages in shallow water, picking food from the surface.
Often goes belly-deep into the water.
(Rooipootelsie)

295

Group 5: Fowl-like birds (gamebirds)

The fowl-like, ground-living birds are well known as many of them are regarded as gamebirds. These are the **francolin, quail, guineafowl** and the more pigeon-like **sandgrouse**.

The most important way to distinguish the different species of **francolin** is by looking at the colour pattern of the underparts. The larger species are characterized by their screeching calls. When approached they usually run away before taking to the wing. The smaller species, often referred to as partridges, have clearer whistling calls. They rely on their camouflaging colours by squatting when disturbed. **Quail** are not often seen as they flush reluctantly.

Guineafowl are characterized by their dark plumage, spotted or streaked with lighter colours.

Sandgrouse are essentially birds of drier regions. They feed on dry seeds, making them very dependent on open water. Flocks congregate daily to drink, but disperse afterwards.

Helmeted Guineafowl

Well known. The bare blue face and neck, red crown and light brown casque are characteristic. The shape of the head casque differs between birds from different parts of its distribution (a and b). (The rarer Crested Guineafowl is darker with a characteristic tuft of head feathers.) Flocks prefer open country: grassland, vleis and farmlands. Scratches for food when foraging. Roosts in trees.
(Gewone tarentaal)

203

12

Crested Guineafowl

The black head plumes are characteristic. Slightly smaller and darker than the Helmeted Guineafowl and with a pale band on the wing. The red eyes are conspicuous on the grey face. The neck and hind part of the head are white. Occurs in denser bushveld, riverine bush and other thickets up to the edge of indigenous forests. Very shy. Sometimes follows monkeys to feed on fruit being dropped.
(Kuifkoptarentaal)

204

5

Namaqua Sandgrouse

The long pointed tail distinguishes both sexes from other sandgrouse. The male's head and breast are yellow brown. He has a double band across the breast, but lacks the banded forehead of the Double-banded Sandgrouse. Females have striped breasts and barred bellies. The Afrikaans name "kelkiewyn" imitates the call. Prefers open stony country with low shrubs and grass. Flocks drink in the early morning.   (Kelkiewyn)

344

Double-banded Sandgrouse

Males have black and white bands on the forehead, a feature which is lacking in male Namaqua Sandgrouse. The double band separates the green-brown breast from the barred belly. Females are paler and are distinguished from female Namaqua Sandgrouse by the barred breast and shorter tail. Found in arid bush and thornveld. Congregate after sunset at waterholes.
(Dubbelbandsandpatrys)

347

Burchell's Sandgrouse

Both sexes are spotted white. The ochre body colour is more yellow on the upperparts. The male's face and throat are grey, while the female's are yellowish. Prefers Kalahari sand and other arid thornveld. Flocks drink in the mornings. Like the Namaqua Sandgrouse, the male saturates his breast feathers to carry water to the chicks in the nest.
(Gevlekte sandpatrys)

345

Crested Francolin

The broad white eyebrow and the triangular dark marks on the breast are characteristic. The black tail is often lifted like that of a bantam. The dark crest is only raised when alarmed. Occurs in bushveld and woodland, preferring areas with dense cover. The call, sounding like "beer and cognac", is given at dusk and dawn. Roosts in trees.
(Bospatrys)

189

Redwing Francolin

The throat is white, but the upper breast is boldly spotted black and white. An orange-brown band extends from the eye down the side of the neck. Occurs in various types of grassland, usually higher on slopes than Shelley's Francolin, but lower down than the very similar Greywing Francolin. Remains still when alarmed, then flies up suddenly on noisy wings. Roosts on the ground.
(Rooivlerkpatrys)

192

Greywing Francolin

The throat is pale grey, spotted with black and bordered with an orange-brown band. The grey belly is finely barred with black. Occurs in montane grassland and scrub, Karoo-like vegetation and coastal fynbos, especially high on mountains and plateaux. Coveys call around dusk from a vantage point, but also when disturbed. Roosts on the ground.
(Bergpatrys)

190

Shelley's Francolin

The breast and flanks are blotched and striped rufous brown. The white throat is bordered with black. There is a white stripe through the eye. The white belly is barred black. Prefers well-grassed areas, especially around stony hills and ridges. The call sounds like "I'll drink yer BEER". Roosts and breeds on the ground in dense grass. More common in the north.
(Laeveldpatrys)

191

Orange River Francolin

The colour varies, the palest occurring in the north-west. The throat is white, bordered with a narrow band of black and white spots. The rufous blotches of the breast extend almost to the white throat and down the sides on the belly. Occurs in arid areas, especially flat stretches, but also on grassy mountain slopes and along pans. Flushes reluctantly, but flies higher than other small francolins.
(Kalaharipatrys)

193

Coqui Francolin

Both sexes have black bands on the breast and belly. The male's golden brown head and neck with a darker crown are characteristic. The female has a white throat bordered with black, white eyebrows and a brown breast. The call is "be-quick" or "co-qui", repeated a number of times. Prefers grassy areas in thornveld or woodland. Walks slowly in a crouched posture. Roosts on the ground.
(Swempie)

188

Harlequin Quail

Males have a white throat with black marks, a dark grey back and chestnut underparts, except for the black breast. (Male Common Quails have pale underparts.) Females are much paler with less prominent facial markings: difficult to distinguish from the female Common Quail. Prefers areas with long grass such as marshes.

Does not flush easily. Flies low, but not far. Nomadic. (Bontkwartel)

201

Natal Francolin

The legs and bill are orange-red, the base of the bill yellow. The feathers on the underparts have white edges, giving a scaled appearance, but the central part of each feather is barred. The upperparts are darker. Occurs in thickets such as riverine bush or rocky hills; also thornveld and coastal dunes. (The similar Red-billed Francolin prefers more arid areas and dry thornveld.) Does not fly far. Roosts in trees. (Natalse fisant)

196

Cape Francolin

The largest francolin in the region. Appears dark at a distance, but the whole body is finely streaked. These stripes are broader and more conspicuous on the underparts. The lower jaw and legs are red. Occurs in coastal and montane fynbos, thickets in kloofs or along river courses. Often calls in the morning and late afternoon. Forages on open patches or farmland. Roosts in trees. (Kaapse fisant)

195

Red-billed Francolin

The orange-red bill and legs, and the yellow eye-ring are characteristic. The pale underparts are finely barred black. The similar Cape and Natal Francolins prefer different habitats. Found in arid riverine bush and other arid thickets, usually in the vicinity of water. The harsh call is often heard especially at dawn and dusk. Forages in open patches. Drinks late afternoon.
(Rooibekfisant)

194

    6

Red-necked Francolin

Like Swainson's Francolin it has a red face and throat. It differs from that species in the completely red bill and legs, and the white stripes on the underparts. Different colour variations occur in different parts of its distribution: (a) in the eastern Cape and (b) in Zimbabwe. Found in denser vegetation than Swainson's Francolin. Shy and wary; keeps near cover. Roosts in trees.
(Rooikeelfisant)

198

      5

Swainson's Francolin

The red throat and eyepatch distinguish it from other francolins except the Red-necked Francolin. The dark legs and bill, and absence of any white on the underparts are characteristic. The body is brown with dark stripes. Found in bushveld with patches of grass and thickets, like riverine bush and vleis. Forages on open patches, sometimes with other francolin. Roosts in trees.
(Bosveldfisant)

199

     6

Group 6: Birds of prey

All birds of prey (also known as raptors) have hooked bills used to tear up their prey. Their eyesight is extremely keen and most have powerful talons to catch prey.

Vultures are huge scavenging birds with bare heads and necks. All true **eagles** have feathered lower legs. Their long broad wings enable them to soar for long periods in search of prey. The **snake eagles** are characterized by their relatively large heads, large yellow eyes and bare legs. **Buzzards** are essentially smaller versions of eagles, but they spend less time flying. Their lower legs are unfeathered. **Sparrowhawks** and **goshawks** are usually inhabitants of wooded areas. Their long legs and tails but short wings give them great manoeuvrability when pursuing prey. **Harriers** frequent open grassland or marshes. The pointed wings of **falcons** and **kestrels** are an adaptation for swift flight enabling them to catch prey on the wing. Kestrels hover regularly.

Their enormous eyes and silent flight enable **owls** to hunt at night.

Cape Vulture

Easily confused with the African White-backed Vulture, but slightly larger and usually much paler. Adults have straw-coloured (not dark) eyes and are generally very pale. Immatures are brown and streaked. The bare neck is bluish in adults, pink in immatures. Adults are mostly seen in the vicinity of mountains where they breed in colonies on cliffs. Immatures venture into open country.
(Kransaasvoël)

122

African White-backed Vulture

The most common vulture in bushveld country. Very similar to the Cape Vulture, but slightly smaller and more brown in colour. The eye is dark. The diagnostic white back of the adult is seen only when the bird spreads its wings. Immatures are streaked. Gathers in large numbers at carcasses where it feeds mostly on the softer parts. Aggressive towards other vultures. Nests in trees, not on cliffs as Cape Vultures.
(Afrikaanse witrugaasvoël)

123

Hooded Vulture

A small brown vulture with a pink face. The back of the head and neck are covered with white down in adults and dark down in immatures. The slender bill indicates that this vulture feeds on scraps left by larger vultures at a carcass. (May be confused with the White-headed Vulture which has a larger bill.) They follow carnivores and are even attracted by their calls. Never found in great numbers.
(Monnikaasvoël)

121

Imm

Ad

Lappet-faced Vulture

A huge, dark vulture. The massive bill and the reddish head are characteristic. Adults have white streaks on the underparts and white feathering on the legs. The brown immatures gradually acquire this colouring. Never numerous at a carcass, but dominates all other vultures on arrival. Feeds on skin and other tough parts of the carcass which other vultures are unable to do. Nests in trees.
(Swartaasvoël)

124

White-headed Vulture

A dark vulture with a white belly. The head is covered with conspicuous white down in adults; brown down in immatures. The bill is red with a blue cere. (The Hooded Vulture's smaller bill lacks the blue cere.) Often the first vulture to arrive at a carcass, but cannot compete as the others gather. Sometimes steals prey from large raptors.
A shy and scantily distributed bird. Usually in pairs.
(Witkopaasvoël)

125

Imm

Ad

Secretary Bird

Unmistakable: the only raptor with very long legs. The long central tail feathers characterize the flight pattern. The adult has a bare orange-red face, while that of the immature is yellow. Forages for small animals by walking slowly across open veld. Seldom flies. In spite of popular belief, snakes form only a small part of its diet. Roosts and breeds on treetops. (Sekretarisvoël)

118

Bateleur

A very colourful raptor with a characteristically short tail. The female has a light grey area at the tip of the folded wing. The immature looks like a Brown Snake Eagle, but has dark eyes and a bare face. The long wings extend beyond the short tail. Spends most of the day in the air, gliding effortlessly. (Berghaan)

♀　　　　　　♂

146

Black Eagle

The magnificent black eagle of mountainous country. The back is white, visible as a "V" when the wings are folded. The immature is mottled brown with a rufous crown and nape. Pairs often soar over their territory. Breeds on edges of cliffs. Its main prey is dassies. (Witkruisarend)

131

Martial Eagle

Africa's largest eagle. It differs from the similar Black-breasted Snake Eagle in its larger size, the feathered legs and the spotted belly. The underwing is dark in flight. The immature is much lighter, has white underparts and a characteristic half-collar. As each pair needs a huge territory (at least 150 km²), this eagle is scantily distributed. Fairly large prey is taken. (Breëkoparend)

140

Crowned Eagle

The large, extremely powerful eagle of our indigenous forests. The crest of longer feathers is not always conspicuous. The underparts are heavily marked. In flight the underwing is rufous in front, the tail is boldly barred. The immature is similar to the immature Martial Eagle, but has more bands across the longer tail and lacks the half-collar. Unobtrusive, but displays above the trees. (Kroonarend)

141

African Fish Eagle

A well-known and unmistakable raptor. The white head, breast and neck distinguish it even at a distance. The immature looks like other brown eagles, but has bare legs and shows the beginning of the white breast. The loud yelping call is often heard near larger bodies of water. The pair spends a lot of time perched in a tall tree. Fish are caught by swooping down and grabbing them in the talons. Nests in trees. (Afrikaanse visarend)

148

53

Long-crested Eagle

A smallish, dark eagle with a characteristic long crest and yellow eyes. The feathers on the lower leg are white in males and brown, off-white or blotched in females. The immature has grey eyes and a shorter crest. Found in the mosaic of taller trees (woodland, forest or plantations) and moist grassland or marshes. Perches conspicuously on telephone poles or on treetops, from where it hunts. Feeds mainly on vlei rats. (Langkuifarend)

139

Brown Snake Eagle

In contrast with true eagles, the snake eagles have unfeathered legs, a large head and large yellow eyes. The adult Brown Snake Eagle is dark brown; the immature is mostly lighter mottled. Prefers dry wooded country (not grassland or thickets) where it is often seen perched prominently on trees. Snakes and other prey are killed and eaten on the ground. Usually solitary, but nomadic. (Bruinslangarend)

142

Imm

Ad

Black-breasted Snake Eagle

Differs from the much larger Martial Eagle by its unfeathered legs and pure white belly. The flight pattern shows white (not dark) underwings. The immature is a rufous brown and gradually acquires the adult plumage. Prefers open country, where it is regularly seen hovering. Smaller prey is eaten in flight. Non-breeding birds may gather in flocks. (Swartborsslangarend)

143

Tawny Eagle

Best distinguished from other common brown eagles by its powerful body: a classic eagle shape. Various colour variations occur (a and b), but most show some tawny (rufous brown) plumage. This versatile bird feeds on a variety of prey including termites; often pirates food from other raptors and is not averse to carrion. Nests in trees. Immatures often occur in flocks. (Roofarend)

132

Wahlberg's Eagle

In summer, this is the most common small brown eagle in the bushveld. Although many colour variations occur (usually dark brown, a, to light brown, b), its slender body shape and long square tail (in flight) may identify it. The head is slightly crested. Often perches in trees and is thus easily overlooked. It draws attention by its whistling call, which is also given in flight. Nests in trees. (Wahlbergse arend)

135

Booted Eagle

This eagle may be distinguished from Wahlberg's Eagle by the thick "booted" appearance of its legs, the light area on the folded wing and the white shoulder patch. The lighter-coloured birds are the most common, although darker variations occur. A widely distributed bird, but more common in the drier western parts of the region. Easily overlooked. Nests on cliffs. (Dwergarend)

136

Yellow-billed Kite

A medium-sized brown raptor with a long forked tail and a yellow bill. The immature has a black bill, but yellow cere. (The bill of the closely related Black Kite is black too, but the bird has a greyish head. Steppe Buzzards have square tails.) A superb flier, continuously twisting its tail to steer. Occurs in large flocks when not breeding. An opportunistic feeder, even taking fish like a fish eagle.
(Geelbekwou)

126b

Lizard Buzzard

A smallish but powerful raptor which could be confused with one of the goshawks or sparrowhawks, or even the Black-shouldered Kite. The vertical black stripe on the throat and the two white bars on the tail are diagnostic. Although it is easily overlooked, it often perches quite conspicuously on a tree. Preys on lizards, insects and other small animals which are caught on the ground.
(Akkedisvalk)

154

Black-shouldered Kite

Probably southern Africa's most common resident raptor. The dark grey back, white underparts and black shoulders make this bird easy to identify. The immature is buffy on the back with the back feathers edged with white. Perches conspicuously on telephone poles and trees, scanning the ground for mice. It hovers regularly before dropping onto the prey. Non-breeding birds roost in colonies.
(Blouvalk)

127

Steppe Buzzard

In summer this is probably the most commonly seen medium-sized brown raptor in the region. Many colour variations occur (a and b). The most distinguishing feature in all but the darkest birds is the pale band across the breast. Immatures have blotched underparts and strongly resemble the rarer Forest Buzzard. It habitually sits on telephone poles and fence posts along the road, especially in open country. (Bruinjakkalsvoël)   149

Eurasia

Jackal Buzzard

A fairly large, almost black raptor. The rufous breast and tail are diagnostic. The broad white band on the underwing is seen while it is soaring overhead in hilly or mountainous country. Immatures have dark brown upperparts and pale brown underparts. Often sits on telephone poles, but is easily overlooked when perched on rocks. Hovers regularly in the wind. Nests on cliff ledges. The call is jackal-like. (Rooiborsjakkalsvoël)   152

1

Augur Buzzard

Resembles the Jackal Buzzard in body shape and habits, but occurs in Zimbabwe and Namibia. In flight the white underparts and underwing (with a dark edge) contrast with the rufous tail. Females have black throats. Immatures have dark brown upperparts and pale underparts. Occurs commonly in mountains and hills. Feeds mainly on snakes and lizards, but also takes other small prey. (Witborsjakkalsvoël)   153

1

Black Sparrowhawk

The largest sparrowhawk in the region. An unmistakable black and white raptor with long yellow legs. In some birds only the throat is white. The underwing and tail are white with black bars. The immature is rufous brown underneath, marked with bold streaks. Like all sparrowhawks, this is a shy and unobtrusive bird. It hides in dense woodland, forest or exotic plantations. Catches birds in flight.
(Swartsperwer)

158

3

African Marsh Harrier

A medium-sized brown raptor with long yellow legs and long narrow wings. The shoulders are blotched with white and a white line borders the facial disc. The immature has a pale bar across the breast. Flies low over marshy areas, holding the wings at an angle above the body and checking the ground for prey (mainly rodents and birds). Nests on the ground in marshes.
(Afrikaanse vleivalk)

165

3

Gymnogene

A fairly large raptor. The plumage is mostly grey, but the belly is barred. The tail is black with a broad white band which is conspicuous in flight. The head is elongated with a bare face which is usually yellow, but changes to red when the bird is excited. Immatures are brown, but can be identified by body and head shape.
Reaches with its long legs into nests or tree holes in search of prey.
(Kaalwangvalk)

169

2

Gabar Goshawk

Very similar to the chanting goshawks, but smaller. The eyes, cere and legs are red. In flight the white rump is seen. Birds with black plumage are sometimes seen. (The black Ovambo sparrowhawk has orange legs and cere.) The immature is more brown, heavily blotched on the paler head and breast, and barred on the belly. Easily overlooked as it perches within the canopy of a tree. Hunts in fairly open country.
(Witkruissperwer)

161

Pale Chanting Goshawk

A fairly large, grey raptor with a finely barred belly. The legs and cere are red. Very similar to the Dark Chanting Goshawk which occurs in the north-eastern parts of southern Africa but has a white rump. Appears almost white in flight, with dark wingtips. The immature is brown with streaked underparts and a white rump. In the dry western parts this bird is conspicuous as it perches on open vantage points.
(Bleeksingvalk)

162

Dark Chanting Goshawk

Very similar to the Pale Chanting Goshawk, but is a darker grey, has a north-easterly distribution. The rump and secondaries are grey, not white as in the previous species. (Also see the Gabar Goshawk on this page.) Immatures have a barred rump, but otherwise are very similar to the immature Pale Chanting Goshawks. Occurs in woodland and savanna. Often perches conspicuously on trees.
(Donkersingvalk)

163

Western Red-footed Kestrel

The male is dark grey with rufous undertail coverts. It could be confused with the Eastern Red-footed Kestrel male, but is darker. The underwing is dark. The female has rufous-brown, slightly streaked underparts. Found commonly in the north-western part of the region. Occurs in large flocks which are most active in the evening. Insects are caught in flight. Roosts in larger trees.
(Westelike rooipootvalk)

179

Eurasia

Eastern Red-footed Kestrel

Similar to the Western Red-footed Kestrel in colour and habits, but with lighter underparts. The female's underparts are blotched. Both sexes have large white areas on the front part of the underwing which are seen in flight. Has a more easterly distribution than the previous species, but is similar in habits. Large flocks roost in trees and perch on telephone lines during the day.
(Oostelike rooipootvalk)

180

 Eastern Asia

Lanner Falcon

A medium-sized raptor with the typical head pattern of a falcon. The rufous crown is diagnostic. The underparts are uniformly pale in adults, but boldly blotched in immatures. The thin moustachial stripe and uniform underparts distinguish it from the Peregrine Falcon. Widely distributed. Has even moved into larger cities, using tall buildings instead of cliffs as nesting sites. Catches birds in flight. Often breeds in the old nests of crows.   (Edelvalk)

172

 4 None

60

Rock Kestrel

A small rufous raptor with a grey head and tail, and spotted upperparts. The female is similar to the male, but is duller and has a barred tail. Could be confused with the Lesser Kestrel (which lacks the spotted upperparts), but it is not a gregarious species. Although occurring in a wide range of habitats, it prefers mountainous and hilly country. Hovers regularly. Breeds mostly on cliff ledges. (Kransvalk)

181

4 **None**

Greater Kestrel

The only kestrel the adult of which has a pale eye. The sexes are similar. The upperparts and flanks are heavily barred, while the underparts are lightly streaked. The immature is similar, but has dark eyes. Favours fairly open, arid country. Sometimes hovers, but is mostly seen sitting on telephone poles or suitable trees from where it hunts. Usually breeds in the nests of crows or other raptors. (Grootrooivalk)

182

4 **None**

Ad

Imm

Lesser Kestrel

This small, very slender kestrel is usually seen in huge flocks during the summer. The underparts are noticeably lighter than the upperparts. The male differs from the similar Rock Kestrel in its unspotted back. The female has spotted upperparts and streaked underparts. Flocks roost in large trees, even in some towns. Perches on telephone lines. Graceful in flight. (Kleinrooivalk)

183

Eurasia

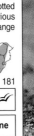

♂

♀

Pygmy Falcon

The smallest diurnal raptor in southern Africa. The white underparts and the white spots on the wings and tail are characteristic. The female is similar to the male, but is more colourful and has a dark chestnut back. This is a bird of the arid west, where pairs often occupy a chamber in the nest of Sociable Weavers. Often seen perched in trees from where they call or survey their surroundings.
(Dwergvalk)

186

  ₃ **None**

Barn Owl

A well-known medium-sized owl which occurs throughout the world. The heart-shaped facial disc, small dark eyes and the slender body characterize this owl. Occurs in a wide variety of habitats and often breeds in old buildings. (The African Grass Owl has darker upperparts, and lives on the ground in moist grassy areas.) The screeching call is a familiar sound in built-up areas. An expert hunter of mice. (Nonnetjie-uil)

392

  ₅ **None**

Marsh Owl

A medium-sized, dark brown owl with slightly pale underparts. As the name indicates, its preferred habitats are marshes, vleis and moist grassland areas. It spends most of the day on the ground, but may perch conspicuously and even fly on overcast days. The long wings are characteristic. Gathers into larger flocks when not breeding. Roosts under tufts of grass. Breeds on the ground.
(Vlei-uil)

395

 ₃

Spotted Eagle Owl

The most common large owl in the region, characterized by its mottled greyish colour, yellow eyes and conspicuous ear tufts. (The rarer Cape Eagle Owl has orange eyes and broader markings on the belly.) Also occurs in urban areas where the typical "hu-hooo" call is often heard. During the day it roosts in trees or among rocks. Breeds in various suitable places. Very adaptable.
(Gevlekte ooruil)

401

None

Giant Eagle Owl

The largest owl in the region. The overall grey colour, dark eyes and pink eyelids identify this bird. The immature is browner than the adult. In spite of its large size it is easily overlooked when roosting in a tree during the day. The call is a deep grunting "hu-hu-hu" or a shrill whistle. Large prey is taken, regularly including hedgehogs. Breeds mostly in other birds' nests.
(Reuse-ooruil)

402

None

White-faced Owl

A smallish owl with a white face bordered by black. (African Scops Owls have grey faces.) The eyes are orange. Hides in trees during the day. Although it is not as well camouflaged as the African Scops Owl, it also elongates its body and closes its eyes when disturbed. Occurs in a variety of wooded areas. The call is a soft "whooo", which is not often heard. Breeds on the nests of other birds.
(Witwanguil)

397

None

Pearl-spotted Owl

The smallest owl in southern Africa. The upperparts and tail are brown, spotted with white. The white underparts are boldly streaked with brown. The back of the head bears two dark eyespots. A bold hunter, often active by day. The call starts with a series of ascending high-pitched whistles. Unlike other small owls, it stares at intruders. Breeds in old barbet or woodpecker nests.
(Witkoluil)

398

African Barred Owl

Very similar to the Pearl-spotted Owl. The white underparts bear brown blotches arranged in rows. (The Pearl-spotted Owl has dark vertical stripes on its underparts.) The head, neck and tail are barred black and white. There is a row of bold white spots on each wing. Occurs in riverine woodland and coastal bush. May hunt during the day, but not as often as the previous species.
(Afrikaanse gebande uil)

399

African Scops Owl

A small greyish or brownish owl with yellow eyes and black spots and stripes. This is the smallest owl with ear tufts in the region. The colour pattern resembles tree bark and lichen. During the day it perches close to a tree trunk, elongating its body and closing its eyes. Then it differs from the White-faced Owl in its grey face. The soft insect-like "prrrrrup" call is often heard in wooded country at night.
(Afrikaanse skopsuil)

396

Group 7: Fruiteaters

The fruiteaters have robust bills enabling them to cut through the skin of fruit and take out large chunks. Smaller fruit or berries are swallowed whole. Insects supplement their diet. Most fruiteaters occur in wooded areas.

Barbets are small colourful birds which breed in self-excavated holes in trees. Their special feet, with two toes pointing forward and two to the back, enable them to cling to the bark of trees.

Parrots and **lovebirds** have stout, hooked bills. Their feet, similar to those of the barbets, and the bill are used to climb around trees.

Louries are crow-sized birds characterized by their long tails and crested heads. Their calls are loud and raucous. The Grey Lourie inhabits more arid country than most louries.

Mousebirds are well-known garden birds. They superficially resemble louries, but are much smaller. They look like mice as they creep along the branches in search of fruit.

Black-collared Barbet

The black collar and the red head and throat are characteristic. The bill is very large. The back is olive-grey and the belly pale yellow. A rare variety has a yellow head and throat. The head and breast of the immature are black, spotted with red. The call is a loud duet. The male and female bob up and down, and open and close their wings while calling. Found in wooded areas, parks and gardens. A group may roost in one nest. (Rooikophoutkapper)

464

Crested Barbet

The black-tipped crest is characteristic. The face and underparts are yellow with red spots. The back, tail and broad breastband are black with white spots. The rump is red. Frequents thickets, riverine bush and gardens. The male's call is a well-known "krrrrrr", sounding like an alarm clock. Jumps around on the ground. More insectivorous than other barbets. Is the breeding host of the Lesser Honeyguide. (Kuifkophoutkapper)

473

Acacia Pied Barbet

The red forehead, yellow eyebrow extending into a white band and the broad black band through the eye are characteristic. The back is pied, the breast white and throat black. (The Red-fronted Tinker Barbet is smaller and lacks the black throat.) The immature has a black forehead. The call resembles that of the African Hoopoe. Found in bushveld, arid scrubland and gardens. Often roosts in other birds' nests. (Bonthoutkapper)

465

Red-fronted Tinker Barbet

The red forehead and golden wing patch are characteristic. The underparts are yellow. (The Yellow-fronted Tinker Barbet may have an orange forehead, but the distribution differs. The larger Acacia Pied Barbet has a black throat.) The immature has a black forehead. Found in coastal bush and dense vegetation. Forages in the canopy where it is seldom seen but often heard. The call is monotonous, similar to that of the next species. (Rooiblestinker)

469

Yellow-fronted Tinker Barbet

The yellow forehead (sometimes orange) and pale yellow underparts are characteristic. (Red-fronted Tinker Barbets have yellower underparts and a different distribution. The larger Acacia Pied Barbet has a black throat and white underparts.) The forehead of the immature is black. Found in broadleaved woodland where it perches high in trees. The call is a monotonous "pink pink pink" similar to that of the previous species. (Geelblestinker)

470

Brown-headed Parrot

This pale green parrot has a brown head and neck, and pale yellow eyes. In flight the bright yellow underwing is seen. (Meyer's Parrot has a yellow forehead and shoulders. The rump and belly are blue-green.) Usually occurs in small flocks. Flies fast and straight. Found in moist broadleaved woodland and riverine bush. Noisy, but not easily seen in the canopy of trees.

(Bruinkoppapegaai)

363

Meyer's Parrot

The blue-green rump, and yellow forehead and shoulders are characteristic. The head, neck, shoulders and tail are brown and the belly green. (The Brown-headed Parrot is more green and lacks the yellow patches. Rüppell's Parrot, in Namibia, has a blue belly.) Found in open woodland, riverine bush and arid bushveld, preferring baobab veld. Shy and wary. Roosts and breeds in tree holes.

(Bosveldpapegaai)

364

Rosy-faced Lovebird

The pink-red face and blue rump are characteristic. The rest of the plumage is green. (The similar Lilian's Lovebird, occuring only along the Zambezi, has a blue rump.) Found in arid areas with trees, usually near water. Drinks regularly. Nests in holes in rock faces or in the nests of Sociable Weavers or Red-billed Buffalo Weavers. The female carries nesting material tucked into the rump feathers.

(Rooiwangparkiet)

367

Knysna Lourie

The green head and crest, white lines around the eyes and the red bill are characteristic. The rest of the plumage is green. The red flight feathers are conspicuous in flight. (The very similar Livingstone's Lourie occurs along the coast north of St Lucia and north of the Limpopo. The Purple-crested Lourie has a purple crest and a dark bill.)

Found in dense forests and coastal bush. Respond to each other's calls.
(Knysnaloerie)

370a

Purple-crested Lourie

Characteristic are the glossy purple crest and the dark bill. The tail and upperwings are blue, the breast and neck olive-yellow to orange-yellow. The red flight feathers are visible in flight. (The Knysna Lourie is greener with a green crest and has a red bill. It prefers moister habitats.) Very shy. Inhabits thickets and dense bushveld. Runs along branches like other louries.
(Bloukuifloerie)

371

Grey Lourie

This well-known bushveld lourie is recognized by its grey plumage, long crest and long tail. The legs and bill are black. Is conspicuous and noisy, especially when alarmed. The characteristic "kwee-h" or "go-away" frustrates many hunters, as it is an alarm call recognized by most animals. Found in more arid areas with trees and in gardens. Often perches on treetops to survey its surroundings. Very alert and wary. (Kwêvoël)

373

Speckled Mousebird

The upper part of the bill is dark while the lower jaw is white. The overall plumage is brownish. The legs are dark and the face black. Inhabits moister areas than the other two mousebirds: forest edges, woodland and gardens. Like all mousebirds, it resembles a mouse while climbing around a tree, hence the name. Flocks fly fast and straight from tree to tree.
(Gevlekte muisvoël)

424

White-backed Mousebird

The head, back and tail are pale grey, the underparts pale brown. (Speckled Mousebirds appear brown.) The rump is white, but this is only characteristic in flight. The bill is white, only the tip of the upper jaw being black. The legs are red. Prefers arid areas: riverine bush, scrub and gardens. Feeds on the ground. Like other mousebirds it loves a dust bath.
(Witkruismuisvoël)

425

Red-faced Mousebird

The bare red cheeks and the blue eyes are characteristic. Is lighter and more blue-grey than the other two mousebirds. More wary than other species. Like other mousebirds it often hangs from a branch, especially when sleeping. Widespread, but prefers dry bushveld with thickets, orchards and gardens. Small flocks fly high from tree to tree. Feeds mostly on fruit.
(Rooiwangmuisvoël)

426

Group 8: Birds with long, straight bills

The **kingfishers, woodpeckers** and **Red-throated Wryneck** are small to medium birds with long, pointed, but straight bills.

Most **kingfishers** are waterbirds. They often sit on overhanging vegetation, diving down to catch fish or other small aquatic animals. Some kingfishers, however, are not associated with water at all. These catch mainly insects or other small animals. All kingfishers are colourful, attractive birds.

Woodpeckers use their bills to chisel away wood in their search of insects. Stiff tail feathers support the body while the bird is pecking. The various species look very similar. Making identification even more difficult is the fact that male and female of a species are often differently coloured and that woodpeckers are shy birds, keeping close to the trunks of trees. They nest in self-excavated holes in trees.

The **Red-throated Wryneck** resembles a woodpecker, but has a shorter bill.

Malachite Kingfisher

A very small kingfisher with a red bill. It has a bright blue back and orange-brown under-parts. (The African Pygmy Kingfisher, a bush-veld bird, has purple ear patches.) The imma-ture has a dark bill similar to the rare Half-collared Kingfisher, but is smaller. Easily overlooked in spite of its bright colours. Found on inland waters, where it perches on low overhanging vegetation. Hunts by diving from its perch. Flies fast and low. (Kuifkopvisvanger)

431

African Pygmy Kingfisher

A very small kingfisher with a red bill. The overall colour pattern is similar to that of the Malachite Kingfisher, but the eyebrow is orange and the ear patches purple. The immature has a black bill. Unlike the Mala-chite Kingfisher, this is a bushveld bird which is usually found away from water. Perches unobtrusively on a low perch and swoops down to the ground to catch prey. (Afrikaanse dwergvisvanger)

432

Woodland Kingfisher

A very attractive turquoise and white king-fisher. The red and black bill and black stripe through the eye are diagnostic. (The entire bill of the rare Mangrove Kingfisher is red.) The immature has a dusky bill and is finely barred. As the name indicates, it occurs in wooded areas away from water. The trilling call "kri-tirrrrrr" is often heard in summer. Perches on the lower branches of a tree from where it hunts.

(Bosveldvisvanger)

433

3

Brown-hooded Kingfisher

Diagnostic are the brown, streaked head and the red bill with its black tip. (The Striped Kingfisher's bill is dark above and red below and it has a white collar.) The male has a black back and wing coverts, while the female's are brown. The immature is duller. Found away from water. Perches conspicuously on fences or branches and is thus often seen. Sometimes dives into water, but this is usually to bathe.

(Bruinkopvisvanger)

435

♂

♀

4

Striped Kingfisher

Smaller than the previous two species and more sombrely coloured. The streaked crown, white neck and the black band through the eye are characteristic. The bill is dark above and red below. (The Woodland Kingfisher's bill colour is the other way round. The Brown-hooded Kingfisher's bill is red with a black tip.) Found away from water in a variety of wooded habitats. Perches low in trees. Noisy when displaying. (Gestreepte visvanger)

437

3

Pied Kingfisher

The only black and white kingfisher in the region. The male is identified by a second, narrower black band across the breast. Found at inland and marine waters. Bold and tame. Often hunts by hovering over the water before diving.

(Bontvisvanger)

428

Giant Kingfisher

The largest kingfisher in the region. The black upperparts are spotted white. The male's breast is brown, the belly whitish; the female's colours on breast and belly are reversed. A shy bird which is easily overlooked unless it is heard calling "wak-wak-wak". Sometimes perches quietly low and over water, both inland and marine. Sometimes hovers. Catches mostly crabs and frogs.

(Reusevisvanger)

429

Red-throated Wryneck

Similar to woodpeckers, but with a shorter bill. The red-brown patch on the throat and upperbreast is diagnostic. The rest of the underparts are whitish with black stripes. A central dark line stretches from the crown to the back. Generally an unobtrusive bird, but often calls, perched conspicuously on an exposed branch. Forages mostly on the ground where it feeds on ants and termites.

(Draaihals)

489

Ground Woodpecker

The largest woodpecker in Africa. The red breast and belly are diagnostic. Males have pink moustachial stripes. The immature is duller than the adult. Found on mountain slopes and rocky outcrops where it often perches prominently. Feeds on ants which are found by foraging on the ground. A shy and wary bird which is difficult to approach. When disturbed the whole flock flies off only to resettle a distance away.
(Grondspeg)

480

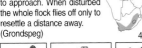

Olive Woodpecker

The only olive-green woodpecker in the region. The crown is red in males, while females have completely grey heads. Both sexes have red rumps which can be seen in flight. Immatures are duller. A forest bird, but it also occurs in riverine bush and coastal thickets or forages in fynbos. Well camouflaged when sitting still. Pairs usually look for food high in large trees, but may come down into small shrubs.
(Gryskopspeg)

488

Bearded Woodpecker

A large woodpecker with barred underparts and a long bill. The moustachial stripes and ear patches are black, while the forecrown is spotted white on black. Males have a red hindcrown; that of the female is black. Prefers drier savanna. The drumming of the bill against dead wood is heard over long distances. Usually occurs in pairs. Searches for insects in rotting wood.
(Baardspeg)

487

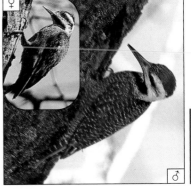

Bennett's Woodpecker

The underparts are spotted (unspotted in Namibia). The male has a red forehead, crown and moustachial stripe. The female has a characteristic brown throat and stripe below the eye; the forecrown is spotted white on black and the hindcrown is red. Forages on the ground where it feeds on ants and termites. Flies into trees at the slightest sign of danger. Prefers used nests of other woodpeckers.
(Bennettse speg)

481

Golden-tailed Woodpecker

The underparts are streaked. The male's forecrown is mottled black on red; the hindcrown and the moustachial stripes are red. The female's forecrown is spotted white on black; the hindcrown is red. Found in a variety of wooded areas. A fairly sparsely distributed, silent and inconspicuous bird. Usually solitary or in pairs. Eats ants and termites, but forages in trees.
(Goudstertspeg)

483

Cardinal Woodpecker

A small woodpecker with a short bill, streaked underparts, black moustachial stripes and a brown forecrown. The hindcrown of the male is red; the female's black. The most common tree-living woodpecker in the region. (The moustachial stripe of the larger Golden-tailed Woodpecker male is red and the female has a red hindcrown.) Feeds on insects and other invertebrates found in dead wood. Often drums its bill against a branch. (Kardinaalspeg)

486

Group 9: Birds with long, decurved bills

The **bee-eaters, hoopoes, wood-hoopoes, hornbills, sugarbirds** and **sunbirds** have long, pointed, but decurved bills. All are medium to small, except the Southern Ground Hornbill which is very large, like a turkey.

The colourful **bee-eaters** hawk bees and stinging insects in the air. In flight they are characterized by their triangular, pointed wings.

The **African Hoopoe**, a well-known garden bird, forages mostly on the ground. The **wood-hoopoes** are tree-living, searching for insects under the bark. They are noisy birds, often occurring in pairs or groups.

The bill of a **hornbill** is surprisingly light in spite of its size. It is usually enlarged by a horny casque, especially in males. The colour of the bill is a good identification guide.

Both **sugarbirds** and **sunbirds** feed on nectar. The iridescent colours of male sunbirds make them very attractive. The females (and non-breeding males of some species) are dull and often difficult to identify. The two species of sugarbirds are larger and less colourful than the sunbirds.

Southern Ground Hornbill

A very large black bird with a large bill. The face and the throat are red. The female differs from the male in having a blue patch on the throat. The white secondaries are visible in flight. The face and throat of the immature are paler, its plumage is brown. The call is a deep booming sound. Found in bushveld with sufficient grass cover. Forages on the ground and digs with its bill for food. Roosts communally in trees. (Bromvoël)

463

Imm
Ad

2

Trumpeter Hornbill

The dark bill with a large casque on top (the female's is smaller) and the pink face are characteristic of this large pied hornbill. The white rump and tips to the secondaries are visible in flight. (The Silvery-cheeked Hornbill is bigger and has a pale bill and blue cheeks.) Found in coastal forests, dense woodland and riverine vegetation. Noisy: the call sounds like a baby crying. (Gewone boskraai)

455

2

Grey Hornbill

The overall grey appearance is characteristic. The male has a dark grey bill; the bill of the female is smaller, tipped with red and the casque on top of the bill is smaller and white in colour. Forages mostly in trees but may catch insects in flight. Pairs or small flocks occur in different types of bushveld. Whistles loudly. Like most other hornbills, the male seals the female into a hollow treetrunk and feeds her while breeding. (Grysneushoringvoël)

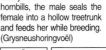

457

Red-billed Hornbill

The fairly slender red bill is characteristic. The back and wings are blotched black and white, the underparts are white. (The other hornbills with red bills are larger and have dark heads and necks.) A bushveld bird, preferring mopane and thornveld. Forages mostly on the ground, digging in the soil or in dung. The male seals the female into the nest and feeds her while breeding. (Rooibekneushoringvoël)

458

Southern Yellow-billed Hornbill

The large yellow bill distinguishes this species from all similar hornbills. The belly is white, the back black with white blotches. This bushveld bird is often seen together with the Red-billed Hornbill, but prefers moister areas. Forages mostly on the ground. During breeding the male seals the female into the nest and feeds her through a narrow slit. (Suidelike geelbekneushoringvoël)

459

Crowned Hornbill

The brown head and upperparts, and the conspicuous casque on the red bill are characteristic. (Red-billed Hornbills have slender bills and white eyebrows. Bradfield's Hornbill, found in the extreme north, has an orange bill without a casque.) Occurs in dense bushveld. Forages in trees. The female is sealed into the nest which is either a hole in a tree or in a rock face.
(Gekroonde neushoringvoël)

460

Bradfield's Hornbill

Although similar to the hornbills with red bills, this hornbill has an orange bill lacking a casque. (The similar Crowned Hornbill's bill has a casque.) There is no white on the wing. The eye is yellow. It is confined to the northern parts where it occurs in woodland and savanna. It lives in pairs when breeding, otherwise in flocks. Forages in trees or on the ground.
(Bradfieldse neushoringvoël)

461

Monteiro's Hornbill

The large red bill and grey-brown breast distinguish it from the Red-billed Hornbill. The wings are marked with small white spots. (Bradfield's Hornbill has an orange bill, brown outer tail feathers and no white on the wings.) Prefers dry hilly thornveld. Frequently perches on top of a large tree. Forages on the ground. Breeds mostly in a hole in a rock face, but also in trees.
(Monteirose neushoringvoël)

462

European Bee-eater

The only bee-eater with a brown back. The yellow throat is bordered with black below, while the blue breast and belly are characteristic. The central tail feathers are elongated. Found in open bushveld, woodland and bushy grasslands. Often perches on telephone wires or dead trees, and catches its prey in flight. Roosts in colonies in trees. Sometimes breeds in southern Africa.
(Europese byvreter)

438

Eurasia

Southern Carmine Bee-eater

The only bee-eater with a red back. The crown and undertail are blue. The rest of the plumage is a characteristic pink-red, darker on the back. The central tail feathers are very long in the adult. The immature is duller and lacks the long central tail feathers. Occurs in woodland and mixed savanna usually near larger rivers. Hunts flying insects over water or near larger mammals. Breeds in colonies in river banks.
(Suidelike rooiborsbyvreter)

441

3

Blue-cheeked Bee-eater

Appears green at a distance but the belly, cheeks, eyebrows and forehead are blue. The throat is brown, merging with yellow towards the chin. (The similar Olive Bee-eater has a brown crown and throat and white eyebrows. It is found only in the extreme north and east.) Usually occurs near large rivers, or in the wooded areas around marshes and pans. Often hunts from a dead tree.
(Blouwangbyvreter)

440

Asia
Africa

White-fronted Bee-eater

Very colourful. The red throat, white chin and forehead are characteristic. The crown and breast are cinnamon. The back and square tail are green. The undertail feathers and the rump are bright blue. The crown and underparts of the immature are green. Common in the bushveld, especially near water. Hunts flying insects in the air or over water. Roosts in trees. Breeds in colonies in sand banks.
(Rooikeelbyvreter)

443

Little Bee-eater

Our smallest bee-eater. The throat is yellow and the breast orange-brown. The black border below the throat is absent in the immature. The back is green; the tail square. (The Swallow-tailed Bee-eater has a blue throat band and a forked tail.) Occurs in different types of bushveld, usually near rivers, open patches and reed beds. Hunts from and returns to a low perch. The nest is excavated in aardvark holes or earth banks. (Kleinbyvreter)

Ad

Imm

444

Swallow-tailed Bee-eater

The blue-green forked tail and underparts are characteristic. The throat is yellow, bordered with blue below. The rest of the body is yellowish green. (Little Bee-eaters have a black band under the throat and orange-brown breasts. Olive Bee-eaters have brown throats and green underparts.) Common in the dry western parts where it frequents thornveld and riverine vegetation. Hunts flying insects from and returns to a perch. (Swaelstertbyvreter)

445

Cape Sugarbird

The male's long tail and bill are characteristic. The back and breast are brown, the throat white with brown moustachial stripes. The tails of females and immatures are shorter. (Gurney's Sugarbird has a rufous crown and breast and lacks the moustachial stripes. The distribution of the two species overlaps only slightly.) Found in fynbos, especially protea veld. The male perches on a tall bush to sing. Breeds during winter.
(Kaapse suikervoël)

773

Gurney's Sugarbird

The rufous crown and breast are characteristic. More brightly coloured than the Cape Sugarbird but lacks the moustachial stripes. The distribution of the two species overlaps only slightly in the eastern Cape. Found in montane scrub with proteas and aloes. Forages for nectar and insects on flowers. The male frequently perches on a tall tree or shrub. Displays by flying steeply into the air and diving down.
(Rooiborssuikervoël)

774

Malachite Sunbird

A large sunbird. The breeding male is glossy green and has a long tail. The female's large size together with the yellow throat and moustachial stripe distinguish her from other sunbirds. The non-breeding male resembles the female although he may retain the long tail and some green blotches on the body. Found in various habitats. Active and aggressive towards other sunbirds.
(Jangroentjie)

775

80

Marico Sunbird

In contrast with the double-collared sunbirds, the male has a wine-red breastband and a dark belly. (The bill is longer and more decurved than that of the Purple-banded Sunbird which is found in the north-east.) The female's underparts are streaked, the belly yellowish. Occurs in thornveld, riverine bush and gardens. Is very active and aggressive towards other sunbirds. (Maricosuikerbekkie)

779

Lesser Double-collared Sunbird

The male double-collared sunbirds have glossy green heads, throats and backs, and red breastbands. In the male Lesser Double-collared Sunbird the breastband is very narrow. (The similar Miombo Double-collared Sunbird is found in Zimbabwe.) The back of the female is brown-grey, the underparts yellow-grey. It hovers often to catch insects in the air or spiders in their webs. (Kleinrooibandsuikerbekkie)

783

Greater Double-collared Sunbird

Males differ from other double-collared sunbirds in their size and broad red breast-bands. (The male Lesser and Miombo Double-collared Sunbirds have narrow breastbands.) The females are larger and have longer bills than those of the other species. Occurs in coastal and riverine bush and montane scrub. Males often call from a prominent perch. (Grootrooibandsuikerbekkie)

785

♂ Nbr

♀

Dusky Sunbird
The breeding male's head, back and breast are black, the belly white. In its non-breeding plumage the upperparts are dark grey and the underparts are white with a black band on the throat and breast. The female resembles the White-bellied Sunbird, but the distribution of the two species differs. Occurs in areas with shrubs, aloes or bushes and trees along river courses. Very active, even in the heat of the day.
(Namakwasuikerbekkie)

788

3

♂

♀

Scarlet-chested Sunbird
The black male's scarlet throat and breast are conspicuous. The chin and forehead are glossy green. The female resembles the Black Sunbird female, but the underparts are more blotched and yellower. Found in bushveld and riverine vegetation. The male is noisy; he often calls from a treetop and even imitates other birds. Aggressive towards other sunbirds and often chases them.
(Rooiborssuikerbekkie)

791

2

♂

♀

African Black Sunbird
The male appears pitch black at a distance, but his forehead is glossy green and the throat and shoulders metallic purple. The female has a pale moustachial stripe, with the underparts more creamy and not as heavily blotched as in the similar Scarlet-chested Sunbird. Solitary or in pairs. Found in bushveld and riverine bush. Hovers over flowers to drink nectar. Can even fly backwards to withdraw its bill.
(Afrikaanse swartsuikerbekkie)

792

2

White-bellied Sunbird

The glossy green head, throat and back, and the blue breastband and white belly of the male are characteristic. The female has brown-grey upperparts and off-white underparts. (Both sexes resemble the Dusky Sunbird which has a westerly distribution. Yellow-bellied Sunbirds, in Zimbabwe, have yellow bellies.) Found in various types of bushveld, often thornveld and riverine bush. Active. Calls often. (Witpenssuikerbekkie)

787

Orange-breasted Sunbird

A well-known sunbird of the Cape fynbos. The male's orange breast and belly, glossy green head and metallic blue breastband are characteristic. The only small sunbird with an elongated tail in this region. The female's underparts are more yellow than in the Lesser Double-collared Sunbird. The male is aggressive towards other birds. Catches prey (spiders and insects) in flight. (Oranjeborssuikerbekkie)

777

Collared Sunbird

A small sunbird with a characteristically short bill. The underparts are yellow, the upperparts green. Males have a completely green head and a blue-purple breastband, and remain brightly coloured throughout the year. Prefers flowering creepers in tall trees or coastal bush. Often joins other birds when foraging. Slits the base of flowers for nectar or feeds on insects and fruit. (Kortbeksuikerbekkie)

793

African Hoopoe

A well-known orange-brown garden bird. The wings and tail are black with white bands (conspicuous in flight). The characteristic long crest is usually folded down, but is erected when the bird is excited. Widely distributed, but prefers wooded areas. Probes with its long slender bill in the soil for food. Its flight is like that of a butterfly. Breeds in a variety of holes and niches in the ground or in tree trunks.
(Afrikaanse hoephoep)

451

Red-billed Wood-hoopoe

Appears dark at a distance, but the plumage is a glossy metallic on the head and upperparts. The red legs and bill are characteristic. (The similar Southern Purple Wood-hoopoe occurs in northern Namibia only. It lacks the glossy green head.) The immature has a dark bill which is not as decurved as that of the Scimitar-billed Wood-hoopoe. Frequents wooded areas. Active and noisy. Flocks look for food under the bark of trees.   (Gewone kakelaar)

452

Scimitar-billed Wood-hoopoe

The black legs and the slender black bill are characteristic. The scimitar-shaped bill is more slender and decurved than those of the immature Red-billed or Southern Purple Wood-hoopoes, which have red legs. The plumage is slightly glossy. Smaller than other wood-hoopoes and occurs mostly in pairs or alone. Found in wooded areas, especially thornveld and riverine vegetation. Feeds quietly on the outer branches. (Swartbekkakelaar)

454

Group 10: Aerial insectivores

Aerial insectivores are characterized by their long, slender wings. Their small bills can open wide to enable them to catch small insects and spiders in flight.

Swallows and **martins** are often confused with **swifts**. **Swallows** and **martins** have angular wings which are easily recognized in flight. Most swallows are colourful and have typical forked tails. The martins are often brownish with square tails.

Swifts are characterized in flight by their sickle-shaped wings. As they have tiny toes, they are not able to perch as most birds do, but cling to vertical surfaces. Swifts are dull-coloured.

Nightjars are often heard at night, but seldom seen. They spend their days on the ground or on a branch where their colour patterns camouflage them effectively. When caught in a spotlight at night their eyes reflect red. The various species look almost identical and are best identified by their different calls.

Little Swift

Like the White-rumped and Horus Swifts, the Little Swift has a white throat and rump. The rump, however, is broad and conspicuous, and the tail is square. (The Horus Swift has a slightly forked tail. The White-rumped Swift has a deeply forked tail and only a narrow white rump.) The nest is a chamber of grass and feathers which are glued together with saliva. Breeds in colonies on cliffs, bridges and tall buildings.
(Kleinwindswael)

417

Unique
2

African Palm Swift

A grey-brown, slender swift with a very long, deeply forked tail. The tail tips are often held together. The slender wings are long and pointed. Is usually found in the vicinity of palms, either indigenous or exotic, even in parks and gardens. Roosts and breeds on the underside of dead palm leaves hanging down, where the nest, a pad of feathers, is glued with saliva.
(Afrikaanse palmwindswael)

421

Unique
2

European Swallow

Differs from other swallows with dark upperparts and deeply forked tails in the rufous forehead and throat, and the broad breastband. The immature may have a white forehead and throat: the broad breastband remains diagnostic. (The White-throated Swallow has a white throat and a narrow breastband.) Prefers farmlands, vleis and open grassland. Large flocks congregate at dusk and in late summer. (Europese swael)

518

Eurasia

White-throated Swallow

The white throat and narrow, dark breastband, together with the rufous forehead distinguish it from other swallows with dark upperparts and deeply forked tails. (The European Swallow has a rufous throat and broad breastband. The Wire-tailed Swallow has an orange-brown cap.) Found over open grassland, usually near water, where it catches insects. The nest is a half-cup of mud and grass. (Witkeelswael)

520

Unique
3

Wire-tailed Swallow

The orange-brown cap, white underparts and long thin tail streamers (which may be temporarily absent) are characteristic. The upperparts are dark metallic blue. (The European Swallow has a brown throat, the White-throated Swallow a white throat. Both have breast bands.) Found near rivers and other water areas in bushveld. Often perches on bridges and railings. The nest, a half-cup of mud, is sometimes built far from water. (Draadstertswael)

522

Unique
3

Red-breasted Swallow

The upperparts, including the cheeks, are dark metallic blue. The underparts are chestnut and the tail is deeply forked. (The Mosque Swallow, which occurs in the north and north-east, has a white throat and cheeks.) Inhabits grassveld, open bushveld and vleis. Flies slower than most swallows and often glides. The nest, a bowl of mud with a tunnel entrance, is built in large holes or pipes.
(Rooiborsswael)

524

Unique
3

Greater Striped Swallow

The two species of striped swallow have dark, metallic blue upperparts, except the rufous rumps and caps. The white underparts are striped finely in the Greater Striped Swallow. These are often not visible in flight. The cheeks are white. Found mostly over open grassy areas; avoids dense bushveld. Forages over water. The flight is relatively slow. The nest is a mud bowl with a tunnel entrance.
(Grootstreepswael)

526

Unique
3

Lesser Striped Swallow

Slightly smaller but similar to the Greater Striped Swallow. The stripes on the underparts are broad and conspicuous, even in flight. The cheeks are rufous like the cap. (The Greater Striped Swallow has finely striped underparts and the cheeks are white with slight stripes.) Prefers woodland and bushveld, but also found in urban areas and grassland. The nest is a mud bowl with a tunnel entrance.
(Kleinstreepswael)

527

Unique
3

87

Pearl-breasted Swallow

The upperparts are dark metallic blue, the tail is forked and the underparts are white. The lack of long tail streamers and any rufous on the head or throat distinguishes it from the European, White-throated and Wire-tailed Swallows. (The House Martin has a white rump.) Found in woodland and arid scrub, near vleis and farmlands. Often perches high on a dead tree. The nest is a half-cup of mud.
(Pêrelborsswael)

523

 Unique 2

Common House Martin

The upperparts are dark blue. The rump and underparts are white, the tail slightly forked. (The Pearl-breasted Swallow has a dark rump and white underwing coverts. The Grey-rumped Swallow, which occurs in the north and north-east, has a grey cap and rump.) Usually occurs near cliffs or high structures such as dam walls and silos. Forages over water, grassland and farmlands. Sometimes breeds here.
(Huisswael)

530

 Eurasia

South African Cliff Swallow

The underparts and forehead are orange-brown. The throat is spotted, with a black band below. The tail is square with a slight notch. The back is dark and the rump brown. Could be confused with the European Swallow which has white underparts. Found in grassland and open bushveld near breeding sites like bridges or buildings. The mud nests are ball-shaped and built close together.
(Familieswael)

528

 Unique 3

Rock Martin

The light brown underparts distinguish it from other martins with brown upperparts. (The Brown-throated Martin has a white belly.) The wings are broad and the white spots on the tail are visible in flight. Common around cliffs, excavations and buildings. Often associates with other swallows and swifts. Flies leisurely with much gliding. The nest is a half-cup of mud.
(Kransswael)

529

Unique
3

Brown-throated Martin

A brown martin with a white belly. Some have brown underparts and are then distinguished from Rock Martins by the absence of white spots on the tail. The tail is slightly forked. (The Banded Martin has a white throat and belly, and a brown breastband.) Usually occurs near water. Often perches on a bush, grass or reeds in the vicinity of water. Breeds during the dry season in colonies in river banks.
(Afrikaanse oewerswael)

533

3

Banded Martin

This brown martin is characterized by the white throat and belly with a broad band across the breast, a short white eyebrow, a square tail and a white area on the under-wing. Flies low and slowly over grasslands while foraging. Often sits on a low perch. Usually occurs alone or in pairs, but flocks gather after the breeding season. Some birds over-winter in especially Botswana and Zimbabwe.
(Gebande oewerswael)

534

3

Freckled Nightjar

This nightjar is associated with rocky hills and koppies, especially granite and sandstone. Here it is so well camouflaged that one nearly steps on it before it flies away. Although one does often see it at dusk in this habitat, it is most easily identified by its call, which sounds like a small dog barking: "bow-how, bow-how". The eggs are laid directly onto the rocks.

(Donkernaguil)

408

None 2

Fiery-necked Nightjar

A common nightjar in bushveld areas and plantations. The characteristic call is often heard at night. It starts with a up-and-down whistle and ends with trilling notes falling in tone; it sounds like "good lord deliver us". The rufous neck of this red-brown nightjar is conspicuous, more so than in other species. (The Rufous-cheeked Nightjar's neck is orange-yellow.) Breeds and roosts on the ground during the day.

(Afrikaanse naguil)

405

None 2

Rufous-cheeked Nightjar

Frequents more open country than the Fiery-necked Nightjar: open thorn- and bushveld, scrub, but also plantations. The characteristic call is heard at dusk (especially at the start of the breeding season): this consists of a number of "awok" sounds followed by a drawn-out "prrrrrrrrrrr", sounding like a small engine. A pale nightjar with an orange neck. Breeds and roosts on the ground during the day.

(Rooiwangnaguil)

406

2 **None**

Group 11a: Insectivores with stout bills

The upper jaw of a typical insectivore's bill is slightly decurved or even hooked at the tip. **Coucals** usually creep through vegetation and are seldom seen flying.

The stout bill of a **shrike** enables it to feed not only on insects, but also to catch small birds or lizards. A large number of shrikes are mostly black and white in colour. The **tchagras** have brown backs and rufous wings. The **bush shrikes** (including the Bokmakierie) are attractively coloured in green and yellow.

Rollers are pigeon-sized bluish birds. They perch quietly for long periods, flying out to catch insects in flight or on the ground. During the breeding season they are noisy and display in a typical rolling, tumbling fashion – hence the name.

Crows and **ravens** are mostly black. Although grouped here with the insectivores, they are omnivorous in their feeding habits and are often seen at carrion. They have heavier bills than the others.

Burchell's Coucal

A conspicuously coloured bird with a long tail. (Other similar species such as the Senegal, Coppery-tailed and White-browed Coucals occur in the northern parts of southern Africa.) The call is a bubbling sound which is often heard on rainy days, hence the name "rainbird". Shy and secretive, creeping through the vegetation. Feeds on garden snails and insects, but also takes nestlings of other birds.

(Gewone vleiloerie)

391a

4

Brubru

A small shrike resembling a batis. The black and white back, white eyebrow and the chestnut flanks are characteristic. The female is browner than the male, especially on her back. Very vocal, singing a duet: the male's call sounds like a telephone; the female's answer is a softer "wheeu". Forages in the canopy of trees and is thus easily overlooked. A very active bird.

(Bontroklaksman)

741

♂

2

Lesser Grey Shrike

Often confused with the Common Fiscal Shrike, but the upperparts are mostly grey. The forehead and ear patches are black. (The Red-backed Shrike's forehead is grey and its back is orange-brown.) The immature is browner on the upperparts and lacks the black forehead. Although widely distributed, it prefers arid country. Perches conspicuously on branches, from where it hunts by dropping onto the prey.
(Gryslaksman)

731

Eurasia

Common Fiscal Shrike

A well-known black and white bird. Could be confused with the smaller Fiscal Flycatcher, but is more stockily built, has a stout bill and a broad white "V" on the back. Western birds have white eyebrows (b). The flanks of females are rufous. The immature is brownish-grey. It is aggressive towards other birds and often chases them.
Perches conspicuously on branches or fence posts.
(Gewone fiskaallaksman)

732

4

Black-backed Puffback

A fairly small, black and white shrike with diagnostic red eyes. The female has a white eyebrow and forehead, and is paler than the male even on the crown. During display the male erects the white feathers on its back, hence the name. Easily overlooked as this is a fairly silent bird which lives high in the canopy of trees. Hops from branch to branch when foraging.
(Swartrugsneeubal)

740

3

92

Southern White-crowned Shrike

A large shrike. The colour pattern of the head is diagnostic (the only shrike with a white forehead and crown). The immature is more brown all over, but shows beginnings of the adult colouration. Prefers acacia savanna, often with baobab trees (hence the Afrikaans name). Groups are very vocal. Perches on the outer branches of a tree.
Feeds on insects, particularly caterpillars.
(Kremetartlaksman)

756

  3

Red-backed Shrike

Although the male resembles other shrikes, the rufous back is diagnostic. (The Lesser Grey Shrike's forehead is black and its back is grey.) The female resembles an immature Common Fiscal Shrike, but is more rufous and without the pale "V" on the back. Widely distributed in wooded areas, but often overlooked in the dry west.
Perches conspicuously, preferring the outer branches of trees or bushes.
(Rooiruglaksman)

733

♂ ♀

  Eurasia

White Helmet Shrike

A pied shrike, characterized by the yellow eye wattle. The upperparts are black (with white wingbars) and the underparts and collar are white. The immature is brownish on the head and lacks the eye wattles. The small flock is closely knit, but includes one breeding pair only. They forage together in all levels of woodland, from the ground to the canopy. Flies in a butterfly-like fashion from one tree to the next.
(Withelmlaksman)

753

  4

Southern Boubou

The cinnamon belly characterizes this large black and white shrike. The breast is sometimes also washed cinnamon. (Other similar boubous have lighter underparts and occur in the northern parts of southern Africa.) A very vocal bird, but many variations of the basic call may be heard. Pairs often call in duet.
Forages in the undergrowth.
A secretive but inquisitive bird.
(Suidelike waterfiskaal)

736

Crimson-breasted Shrike

The crimson underparts and the white wingbar on the black upperparts make this bird unmistakable. The immature has grey underparts. Most common in the drier west where it prefers areas with thorn trees. Runs around like a thrush. Usually forages on the ground, but also in trees. Pairs often call in duet and are more often heard than seen. A fairly secretive but inquisitive bird.
(Rooiborslaksman)

739

African Long-tailed Shrike

The only shrike with a very long tail. The white "V" on the back contrasts boldly with the black body. In flight the white patches on the wings are conspicuous. Females have white patches on the flanks. The immature is browner overall. Occurs in small groups and prefers open savanna where it perches on the top or on side branches of trees. Hunts by dropping onto prey, which consists mostly of insects.
(Afrikaanse langstertlaksman)

735

Southern Tchagra

The three species of tchagra on this page are very similar, but the rufous-brown crown of the Southern Tchagra is diagnostic. (The Three-streaked Tchagra's crown is edged in black.) The immature is similar to but duller than the adult. Less common in the north of its distribution. A shy and secretive bird, foraging in the undergrowth of dense thickets on the edge of forests. The call is a loud trill. (Grysborstjagra)

742

Three-streaked Tchagra

Slightly smaller than the other two tchagras on this page. The crown is light brown with black edges. The white eyebrow is edged above and below in black, hence the name. Found in much the same areas as the Black-crowned Tchagra, but prefers thornveld. Usually solitary or in pairs. Forages mostly on the ground or low down in shrubs. The male displays in flight above the trees. (Rooivlerktjagra)

743

Black-crowned Tchagra

Very similar to the Southern Tchagra, but the crown is black. (The distribution areas of the two species overlap only slightly.) The immature is duller than the adult is, the crown is mottled brown and black, and the bill is horn-coloured. Usually solitary or in pairs. The call sounds like a drunk person whistling on his way home. Secretive and wary, foraging near the ground in wooded areas. (Swartkroontjagra)

744

Bokmakierie

The underparts are yellow; the throat is bordered with a black band, but this feature is absent in the immature. (Might be mistaken for the Yellow-throated Longclaw which has brownish upperparts.) The yellow-tipped tail is clearly visible in flight. The name is derived from the call which, however, is very variable.
Forages in the undergrowth of trees and in thickets.
(Bokmakierie)

746

Orange-breasted Bush Shrike

The underparts are yellow with an orange breast. Could be confused with other bush shrikes, but the forehead and eyebrow are yellow, the crown and nape grey, and the ear patches black. The immature lacks the orange breast and black ear patches. Occurs in dense bush or edges of forest. Although not secretive it is more often heard than seen.
(Oranjeborsboslaksman)

748

Grey-headed Bush Shrike

A large bush shrike (the largest in Africa), with no black on its face. The heavy black bill and yellow eyes are diagnostic. The immature has a horn-coloured bill. A secretive bird which is more often heard than seen. The call is a ghostly "whooo", hence the Afrikaans name meaning "ghostbird". Forages mostly in the lower canopy of trees, but may also come down into the undergrowth.
(Spookvoël)

751

European Roller

Most of the body is pale blue, but the upper-parts are mostly brown. The tail is rounded. The immature is tinged with brown on the head and breast. Although widely distributed, this roller is most common in the western arid regions. Prefers open savanna or grassland with scattered trees. Perches conspicuously on trees and telephone poles from where it glides down to catch insects on the ground. Normally silent.
(Europese troupant)

446

Eurasia

Lilac-breasted Roller

Very colourful: the lilac breast, contrasting with the blue underparts and greenish nape, is diagnostic. The outer tail feathers are long and slender, but are absent in the duller immature and moulting birds. (The Racket-tailed Roller has broadened tips to these feathers and blue underparts.) Perches boldly on telephone poles or trees. Raucous calls and the tumbling display flight indicate the breeding season.
(Gewone troupant)

447

3

Purple Roller

A large, dull-coloured roller. The white eye-brow, rounded tail and the white streaks on the purple underparts are diagnostic. (The European Roller, which also has a rounded tail, has blue underparts and head.) The immature is even duller. This is the only roller to be seen in semi-desert regions, but it usually prefers savanna. Although it is less active, the behaviour is much the same as that of the other rollers.
(Groottroupant)

449

3

Black Crow

A completely black, slenderly built crow. The immature is brownish. Not as bold as the other crows. The usual call is a harsh "khraaa". Usually in pairs. Prefers open areas and also found in very dry country. Perches conspicuously on trees and telephone poles. Not to be confused with the House Crow (with a dark grey breast and neck), a smaller exotic species introduced to Durban. (Swartkraai)

547

Pied Crow

The white breast and collar around the neck identify this crow. (Only the neck of the White-necked Raven is white.) The immature is duller. Like other crows it also imitates other sounds, but the usual call is a harsh croak. This crow is widely distributed, often occurring in urban areas and generally associating with humans. Flies with slow wing beats. Roosts in huge flocks in trees. (Witborskraai)

548

White-necked Raven

The largest crow in the region. Unlike the Pied Crow it lacks the white breast and only the back of the neck is white. The bill is extremely heavy and tipped with white. The wings are broad. The immature is browner. The usual habitat is mountains, but it may forage in adjacent areas. An excellent flier, soaring up and down cliffs and generally playing in the wind. Usually solitary or in pairs. (Withalskraai)

550

Group 11b: Insectivores with medium-sized bills

The slightly decurved upper bill is typical of these birds. Most are small to medium in size, their bills resembling those of thrushes. This is an extremely large and diverse group.

Cuckoos are more often heard than seen. Their monotonous calls are easily identified. **Larks, pipits** and **longclaws** are ground-living, well camouflaged birds. The identification of the different species is often problematic, but is facilitated by listening to their calls. **Wagtails** usually occur near water. Their bright yellow colours make **orioles** very conspicuous. Just like the **bulbuls** they also feed on fruit. Attention is drawn to flocks of **babblers** by their incessant calling. **Thrushes, chats** and **robins** are tree-living birds which often forage on the ground. Many **flycatchers** hawk insects in the air. They are quiet, gentle birds. The **batises** are small, robust flycatchers with brightly coloured plumage. The plumage of the omnivorous **starlings** is iridescent, the colour changing according to light conditions.

Greater Honeyguide

The male is distinguished by the black throat, pink bill and large white ear patch, but the female is a fairly nondescript bird. Both sexes have a yellow shoulder patch, although it may be inconspicuous. Immatures have yellowish underparts. Sometimes guides humans to bees' nests with a rattling guiding call. Otherwise the male calls "vic-torr". Parasitises various hole-nesting birds like bee-eaters and kingfishers.
(Grootheuningwyser)

474

	Breeding parasite

Lesser Honeyguide

Nondescript: olive-grey upperparts and grey belly. The bill is short but thick. The characteristic white outer tail feathers are shown in flight. Easily identified by its call: a monotonous series of "krrr krrr" notes which can be heard some distance away. Does not guide humans to bees like the Greater Honeyguide. Parasitises mainly the Black-collared, Crested, Acacia Pied and White-eared Barbets.
(Kleinheuningwyser)

476

	Breeding parasite

African Cuckoo

A grey cuckoo with a barred breast and belly. May be confused with the European Cuckoo (a non-breeding summer visitor), but its bill is mainly yellow and the underside of the tail is barred, not spotted. Secretive; it is more often heard than seen. The call is "hooop-hooop", like that of the African Hoopoe, but more drawn out. Flies low from tree to tree when approached. Brood parasite of the Fork-tailed Drongo.
(Afrikaanse koekoek)

375

Breeding parasite

Red-chested Cuckoo

Distinguished from the African Cuckoo by its dark grey upperparts, rufous breast and the dark eyes. The male's call is well known, giving rise to the Afrikaans name: "piet-my-vrou". Calls from a specific post, even at night, but is not often seen as it perches inside the canopy of trees. Hawk-like in flight. Lays its eggs in the nests of robins, thrushes, flycatchers, wagtails and some other hosts.
(Piet-my-vrou)

377

Breeding parasite

Diederik Cuckoo

The glossy green upperparts may appear dark at a distance. The red eye, prominently barred flanks and white spots on the wings distinguish this species. The female is more coppery on the back. The immature has a brown, streaked head and a red bill. The male calls from the top of a tree: the name imitates the call. Brood parasite of various seed-eaters, such as sparrows, weavers and bishops.
(Diederikkie)

386

Breeding parasite

Great Spotted Cuckoo

Distinguished by its grey, crested head, dark upperparts spotted with white, and light underparts. The immature is browner with a smaller black crest. The male is very noisy and conspicuous at the beginning of the breeding season, when it often calls from the top of a tree. Otherwise secretive, keeping to cover, but may forage on the ground. Brood parasite of crows and starlings.
(Gevlekte koekoek)

380

Breeding parasite

Jacobin Cuckoo

The black upperparts, white underparts and crested head characterize this cuckoo. (Similar to the Striped Cuckoo which has a finely streaked breast.) A rare black form with only a white wingbar is found as well. Not as secretive as most other large cuckoos. Is active and very noisy at the beginning of the breeding season. Parasitises mainly bulbuls and the Common Fiscal Shrike.
(Bontnuwejaarsvoël)

382

Breeding parasite

Black Cuckoo

Appears entirely black at a distance. Unlike the black form of the Jacobin Cuckoo it has no crest. Usually solitary. An extremely secretive bird, keeping to thick cover in the canopy of trees. The monotonous call, however, is often heard: a three-note whistle, with the first two short and the last one long and rising in pitch: "I'm-so-saad". Parasitises Fork-tailed Drongos, Crimson-breasted Shrikes and boubous.
(Swartkoekoek)

378

Breeding parasite

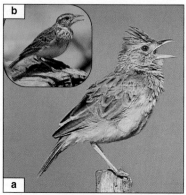

Rufous-naped Lark

The most common lark in the region. Best identified by its call, a characteristic "tireee tireooo" given from a prominent perch like a fence post, low bush or rock while raising its crest. A large, fairly robustly built lark. The red on its neck is seldom seen. Shows red on wings while flying. Various colour forms exist (a and b). Fairly tame and difficult to flush. Prefers open areas with a few bushes or trees.
(Rooineklewerik)

494

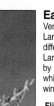

Eastern Clapper Lark

Very similar to the Cape and Agulhas Clapper Larks which have a similar flight display, but differ in distribution. Also similar to the Flappet Lark (more greyish), but best distinguished by the distribution and flight display, during which the lark flies up into the air flapping its wings, then descends rapidly while whistling.
(Hoëveldklappertjie)

Flight display

495b

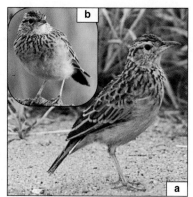

Flappet Lark

Similar to the clapper larks, but differs in distribution and the flight display which is performed very high above the ground, alternately flapping its wings noisily and gliding silently. The colour pattern varies a lot (a and b), the palest forms occuring in the north-west.
(Laeveldklappertjie)

Flight display

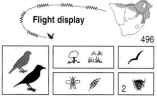

496

Sabota Lark

A very common lark in the drier savanna areas. The distinctive broad eyebrow and the underparts are white, the breast boldly striped black. The pattern on the cheeks is diagnostic. The bill is fairly heavy, shaped like a dagger, but visibly larger in western birds (b). Forages on the ground, but sings mostly from a tree. The call is variable and includes imitations of other birds and even mammals.

(Sabotalewerik)

498

Southern Thick-billed Lark

A stoutly built lark. The bill is large and heavy with a yellow base. The underparts are boldly marked and the tail is short. The crest is raised while the bird is singing or when alarmed. Prefers open areas such as grassland, Karoo, low fynbos or agricultural lands. Is often seen on the grassy verges of roads. The attractive call is uttered from a perch or during the display flight.

(Suidelike dikbeklewerik)

512

Red-capped Lark

A pipit-like lark. The red crown and the red shoulder patches make it easy to identify. The underparts are off-white without any markings. It calls mostly from the ground, but also during the twisting display flight. The call is a jumbled trilling, often interspersed with imitated calls of other birds. Flocks occur in open areas with short or no grass.

(Rooikoplewerik)

507

103

Spike-heeled Lark

This medium-sized lark has a fairly long bill, but is distinguished from the similar Long-billed Lark by the rufous underparts and the short tail with a white tip. It normally assumes a very erect posture. Variable in colour (a and b): the palest forms occur in the arid west. Usually in pairs or small groups. Forages on the ground and only flies when disturbed. The call is a musical trill.
(Vlaktelewerik)

506

Chestnut-backed Finch-lark

The chestnut back of both sexes is diagnostic. The whole crown of the male is black. (The Grey-backed Finch-lark male is more greyish with a white hindcrown.) The female is darker than the Grey-backed Finch-lark female with a pale collar on the hindneck. Large flocks form in the non-breeding season. Prefers bare open areas where it forages on the ground. Flies low and lands suddenly.
(Rooiruglewerik)

515

Grey-backed Finch-lark

Both male and female have grey upperparts. The male has a white patch on the crown. (The Chestnut-backed Finch-lark male's crown is black and its back is more reddish brown.) The female is lighter than that of the previous species. Although the two finchlarks have similar habits and are often found in much the same habitat, the Grey-backed Finch-lark prefers drier areas.
(Grysruglewerik)

516

Eastern Long-billed Lark

A large lark with white or buff underparts, a long bill and a fairly long tail. The colour of this species varies. Very similar to the other four long-billed larks with different areas of distribution. It could also be confused with the Spike-heeled Lark. Has a typical crouched posture when searching for food with its bill. Males call "peeeeeo" during the vertical display flight.
(Grasveldlangbeklewerik)

500a

Grassveld Pipit

The pipits are among the most difficult birds to identify in the field, but the Grassveld Pipit is the most widespread and common. Its head and back have generally more stripes, the breast more distinct spots and the belly more white than in similar pipits. The base of the bill is yellow and the outer tail feathers white. It prefers grassland or grassy areas in savanna. Wags its tail after running a short distance.
(Gewone koester)

716

Long-billed Pipit

Similar to the Grassveld Pipit, but is more grey-brown (less striped) above. The underparts are more dull-brown and the outer tail feathers are buff (not white). The moustachial stripes are usually more distinct. The base of the bill is pink. Prefers hilly areas where it is found in grassy and shrubby patches between rocks. Does not wag its tail as the Grassveld Pipit does.
(Nicholsonse koester)

717

Orange-throated Longclaw

The orange throat bordered with black and the orange-yellow underparts distinguish this bird. The patch on the female's throat is paler and the breastband thinner. The immature has an ochre-buff throat and an incomplete gorget. The tail has a white tip. The typical call is a catlike "meew". This ground-living longclaw prefers short grasslands, often in the vicinity of vleis. Sometimes perches on a low shrub or mound.
(Oranjekeelkalkoentjie)

727

African Pied Wagtail

Similar to the Cape Wagtail in body shape and colouring, but this is a boldly pied (black-and-white) bird. The underparts, throat and eyebrow are white; on the breast is a black band. The immature is brown and white. Prefers the shores of rivers and dams, although it also occurs in gardens, especially in the north. The habits of this tame and trusting bird are very similar to those of the Cape Wagtail.
(Afrikaanse bontkwikkie)

711

Cape Wagtail

A well-known garden bird. Its head and upperparts are grey, the throat is white with a grey breastband across the grey-white underparts. It lacks the white wingbar of the African Pied Wagtail. The white outer tail feathers are shown in flight. The call is a whistling "twee". It also frequents the shores of streams, ponds and dams. It has a characteristic way of walking about briskly and wagging its tail from time to time.
(Gewone kwikkie)

713

Yellow-throated Longclaw

In contrast with the Orange-throated Long-claw, it has completely yellow (not orange-yellow) eyebrow and underparts except for the black gorget. The brown upperparts distinguish it from the Bokmakierie (a shrike with a grey-green back). The immature has an incomplete gorget. Prefers moist areas with rank grass and vleis. Although it also forages on the ground, it perches on trees or bushes when disturbed.
(Geelkeelkalkoentjie)

728

African Yellow-bellied Bulbul

This bulbul's bright yellow underparts and dark red eyes with white eyelids are characteristic. The upperparts are dull greenish. (The Sombre Bulbul is olive-green with characteristic white eyes.) Noisy while foraging for food low in bushes or on the ground. Frequents coastal and riverine bush, as well as well-vegetated rocky hills. More numerous in moister areas.
(Geelborswillie)

574

Sombre Bulbul

A nondescript, olive-green bird characterized by its white eyes. (The African Yellow-bellied Bulbul has dark red eyes.) Not often seen, but the call is a familiar sound in the forest and bush of the east and south coast. The usual call is a penetrating "willie". The territorial call is described as "Willie, come-and-have-a-fight, scaaared".
Keeps to the cover of the tree canopy where it is well camouflaged.
(Gewone willie)

572

Cape Bulbul

The Cape Bulbul is the darkest of three very similar species of bulbul whose areas of distribution overlap only slightly. All three have yellow feathers under the tail, a darker crested head and a darker tail. The Cape Bulbul's white eye-ring is diagnostic. (Those of the other two species on this page are either black or red.) It occurs in fynbos, but also enters stands of exotic trees and gardens.

(Kaapse tiptol)

566

African Red-eyed Bulbul

The red eye-ring of this bulbul is diagnostic. Its white belly contrasts with the darker breast and head (more so than in the Black-eyed Bulbul). The immature is duller and has a pink eye-ring. This is a bulbul of the arid western parts of the region, but it is nearly always found in the vicinity of water. Like the other bulbuls it feeds on fruit, nectar and insects. Its habits are similar to those of the next species.

(Afrikaanse rooioogtiptol)

567

Black-eyed Bulbul

In contrast with the previous two bulbuls, this species has a black eye-ring. It occurs in the moister eastern half of the region. The liquid call is often heard in gardens and woodland. A conspicuous, restless bird, often perching on the top of a tree to sing. Forages mostly in trees, but also on the ground and even catches insects in flight. Is usually the first bird to sound the alarm for a snake or owl.

(Swartoogtiptol)

568

Southern Pied Babbler

White all over except for the black wings, tail and bill. The eyes are yellow to orange. The immature resembles the immature Arrow-marked Babbler. Flocks are conspicuous: the call is similar to that of the next species. This babbler occurs in the drier savanna. It forages mostly on the ground, hopping around or searching like a thrush in leaf litter for insects. (Witkatlagter)

563

Arrow-marked Babbler

The white arrow-like streaks on the underparts are diagnostic. The eye is a conspicuous orange. (The Black-faced Babbler has yellow eyes and the Hartlaub's Babbler has a white rump.) The immature lacks the streaks on the underparts and has brown eyes. The call of this noisy bird is similar to that of the Red-billed Wood-hoopoe, but is not as harsh. Flocks usually forage in the lower canopy of trees, in bushes and on the ground. (Pylvlekkatlagter)

560

Grassbird

Similar to but larger than the cisticolas. The rufous colour, mottled back and streaked underparts distinguish it from the rare localized Moustached Warbler. The sexes are alike. Frequents areas of tall grass, bracken fern or other rank vegetation. Often perches prominently while singing or sunbathing. Usually singly or sometimes in pairs. (Grasvoël)

661

Karoo Thrush

It is distinguished from the similar Kurrichane Thrush by the yellow bill and the speckled throat. (The similar Olive Thrush has orange underparts and occurs in moister habitats in the east and south.) Commonly found in gardens. Forages by scratching in leaf litter found on the ground. Tame in gardens, but otherwise shy.
(Bruinlyster)

577b

Kurrichane Thrush

Similar to the Olive and Karoo Thrushes, but distinguished by its bright orange-red bill and white throat with distinct black stripes. The belly is white. (The Olive and Karoo Thrushes have yellow bills and fine speckles on the throat.) Found in a variety of wooded habitats. Often enters gardens where it becomes tame and trusting. Forages on the ground. Leans forward when running, but stands erect.
(Rooibeklyster)

576

Groundscraper Thrush

The upperparts are brown-grey and the white underparts are marked with black spots and blotches. (The rare Spotted Thrush inhabits forests and has white spots on the wing.) Frequents bare areas within its wooded habitat. A bold but wary bird. Stands very upright. Habitually flicks one wing at a time. Gathers in loose flocks when not breeding. The call is "litsitsirupa", the same as the scientific and Tswana names.
(Gevlekte lyster)

580

Cape Rock Thrush

The different species of rock thrush are very similar. Only the head of the male Cape Rock Thrush is grey. (The other species' upperparts are also grey.) The female is more richly coloured than those of the other species. Found in rocky areas like mountain slopes and gorges, even coming into suburbs. Often perches on rocks, but is easily overlooked. Nests mostly on the ground.
(Kaapse kliplyster)

581

Sentinel Rock Thrush

The head, breast and upperparts of the male are grey. The female's head, breast and back are brown, mottled with white. (The female Cape Rock Thrush has a plain brown breast.) Favours open hilly grassland with rocky outcrops and ridges. May enter human settlements if the habitat is suitable. Forages on the ground by scuttling and hopping around very actively. Often perches on rocks to survey the surroundings.
(Langtoonkliplyster)

582

Short-toed Rock Thrush

Resembles the Sentinel Rock Thrush, but the distributions do not overlap. The male's crown is whitish; the rest of the head and the upperparts are grey. The female has a white throat mottled with brown, but whiter than that of other female rock thrushes. Frequents rocky hills covered with bushes or small trees. Although it is mostly seen on the ground, it readily perches in trees.
(Korttoonkliplyster)

583

Natal Robin

The orange underparts, including the face, distinguish this bird from other robins. The back is a characteristic metallic blue-grey. Inhabits dense vegetation like forests or riverine growth, but is also a well-known garden bird. Forages on the ground. It is seldom seen except at dusk when it comes into the open. Imitates a wide variety of sounds, from bird calls to telephones and dogs. (Nataljanfrederik)

600

Heuglin's Robin

May be confused with the Cape Robin, but the completely orange underparts are characteristic. (The similar Natal Robin has neither a black cap nor white eyebrows. The Chorister Robin lacks white eyebrows.) Like most of the colourful robins, this is a shy bird keeping to dense vegetation. In Zimbabwe, however, it is found in some gardens. The call is "think-of-it", repeated several times. (Heuglinse janfrederik)

599

Cape Robin

A number of colourful robins have black caps and white eyebrows. The Cape Robin is distinguished by its grey belly and orange breast. (The underparts of the similar Heuglin's Robin are completely orange.) Inhabits dense vegetation like forest edges, riverine thickets and gardens. A secretive bird, but is more often seen at dusk when it forages in the open. Sometimes calls from an exposed perch. (Gewone janfrederik)

601

112

African White-throated Robin

Similar to the Cape Robin, but the white throat, breast and wingbars are clearly visible. The flanks and feathers under the tail are orange. This robin is found in dry bushveld, but usually keeps to dense thickets and riverine bush. Seldom seen. Like other robins it forages on the ground, hopping around actively. Sings well and imitates the calls of other birds.
(Afrikaanse witkeeljanfrederik)

602

Familiar Chat

A brown nondescript chat which is difficult to identify when perched. In flight the rufous rump and outer tail feathers are diagnostic. (The similar Sickle-winged Chat has lighter underparts, is more robustly built and has a rufous rump only. Found mostly in Karoo and montane grassland areas.) Perches conspicuously and often flicks its wings in a characteristic manner. A tame bird.
(Gewone spekvreter)

589

Tractrac Chat

Shows a similar behavior to the previous species, but is much paler, especially birds from the Namib. The rump and the outer tail feathers are white. (The Karoo Chat is similar, but is larger and more slenderly built and usually has a grey rump.) Perches conspicuously on bushes and rocks in open scrub, but runs around on the ground while foraging. Flicks its wings similarly to the Familiar Chat.
(Woestynspekvreter)

590

White-browed Robin

This brownish robin is distinguished by the bold white pattern on the wing and the streaked breast. The darker tail has a white tip which is seen in flight. (The Kalahari Robin has no streaks on the breast.) Found widely in wooded areas, but is secretive and thus not often seen. Keeps to bushes and other small thickets. Sings from within this cover. Often holds its tail upright like a prinia. (Gestreepte wipstert)

613

Karoo Robin

The various brownish robins with white eyebrows are very similar, but this is the drabbest of them all. It usually inhabits Karoo veld. It moves, however, into adjacent habitats in times of drought and might then be found with the Kalahari Robin, which is lighter with an orange tail. A conspicuous bird which often calls and scolds from the top of a bush. (Slangverklikker)

614

Kalahari Robin

Similar to the Karoo Robin. The pale sandy colour and the tail which is rufous, edged first with a black band and ending in a white tip (seen when the tail is spread) are characteristic. Inhabits thornveld and scrub, especially in areas with bare ground. Forages on the ground, but calls perched on top of or from the cover of a bush. Like most other robins it also flicks its tail. (Kalahariwipstert)

615

114

Mountain Chat

Both sexes have white rumps and outer tail feathers which are conspicuous in flight. The male is either grey (a) or black (b), with characteristic white shoulder patches. A black male usually has a grey crown. Females are black or dark brown. Found in rocky grasslands with termite mounds and on mountain slopes. It also adapts to urban areas. An active bird which flies from rock to rock while foraging.
(Bergwagter)   586

Capped Wheatear

A characteristically coloured ground-living bird. The immature is browner and lacks the black breastband. (The Buff-streaked Chat has white shoulders and a black throat.) Favours open country, where it is often seen perched on rocks or termite mounds in a very upright fashion. Forages actively, often flicking its wings and jerking its tail. Imitates various sounds. Nests in the burrows of rodents.
(Hoëveldskaapwagter)   587

Southern Ant-eating Chat

This dark brown chat appears black from a distance, has a characteristic upright posture and a short tail. The male has a white shoulder patch, but this is not always visible. The white wingtips are conspicuous in the fluttering flight. Ground-living, but is often seen perched on termite mounds, rocks, bushes or fences along the road. Excavates a nest in a sand bank or in the roof of an aardvark hole.
(Suidelike swartpiek)   595

Mocking Chat

The male's colour pattern is characteristic: black with an orange-brown belly and white wingbars. The female is slaty black, except for the red-brown belly and thus less easy to identify. Occurs in a variety of rocky but well-wooded habitats. The male is fairly conspicuous, perching on boulders or in trees. Imitates the calls of other birds. Usually breeds in the nest of the Lesser Striped Swallow.
(Dassievoël)

593

Cape Rockjumper

The male is unmistakable. The female is similar, but much paler underneath and lacks the black throat and cheeks. (Could be confused with the Orange-breasted Rockjumper which is much paler underneath and occurs above 1000 m in the Drakensberg and Eastern Cape; their distributions however do not overlap.) Occurs in pairs or small flocks. Inhabits rocky mountain slopes where it perches conspicuously.
(Kaapse berglyster)

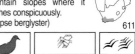

611

Common Stonechat

A small robust chat. The male is easy to identify: the breast is reddish-brown, the head and throat are black and there are white patches on the sides of the neck. The female has a pale brown head and upperparts, while the underparts are cinnamon. Both sexes have white rumps and wing patches which are conspicuous in flight.
Inhabits open grassland, in the vicinity of water. Perches conspicuously.
(Gewone bontrokkie)

596

Pririt Batis

Batises are small, attractively coloured fly-catchers. The male Pririt Batis is very similar to the Chinspot Batis male, but their distribution areas do not overlap. The female is yellow-brown on the throat and breast. (The Cape and Chinspot Batis females have brown breastbands.) Batises are lively birds, gleaning insects from foliage.

The Pririt Batis often occurs in the trees along rivers. (Priritbosbontrokkie)

703

Chinspot Batis

The male Chinspot Batis is very similar to the Pririt Batis male, but occurs more to the east. The female has a brown breastband and a characteristic small brown spot on the throat. Inhabits bushveld, woodland and riverine thickets. (The more richly coloured Cape Batis is a forest bird.) Similar to other batises in habits. Displays actively above trees and other open spaces. (Witliesbosbontrokkie)

701

Cape Batis

The male is distinguished from other batis males by its broad black breastband, the rufous flanks and wingbar and the absence of a white eyebrow. The female is similar, but has a chestnut breastband, short white eyebrows and a rufous throat. Occurs mainly in forests and plantations, although it may forage more widely in surrounding areas in winter. A tame bird. (Kaapse bosbontrokkie)

700

Black Cuckoo-shrike

The male differs from other similar blackish birds in that it has an orange gape and a rounded tail. A yellow shoulder patch may be present or absent. The variegated female is yellowish with lighter barred underparts (as shown) and appears more cuckoo-like. An unobtrusive bird which perches quietly in the canopy of woodland trees. Often joins other birds while foraging.
(Swartkatakoeroe)

538

Fork-tailed Drongo

The deeply forked tail and red eyes of this black bird are diagnostic. Well known and widely distributed; found wherever there are trees, but is most common in bushveld. (The smaller Square-tailed Drongo has a slightly notched tail and inhabits forests. The Southern Black Flycatcher's tail is more square.) Perches prominently on a vantage point. Catches insects in swift flight or on the ground. Noisy.
(Mikstertbyvanger)

541

Eastern Black-headed Oriole

A striking yellow bird with a black head and upper breast, and a characteristic red bill. The immature is duller in colour, the head streaked with yellow. The call, which is often heard, is loud and liquid. It forages mostly in the canopy of larger trees and is frequently seen flying from one tree to the next. A conspicuous and attractive garden bird.
(Oostelike swartkopwielewaal)

545

Southern Black Flycatcher

Distinguished from similar black birds by the square tail (only slightly notched) and the straight tail feathers. Its eyes are dark, not red like the Fork-tailed Drongo's. Inhabits a variety of wooded areas, including gardens. The habits are typical of a flycatcher. Sometimes behaves like the Fork-tailed Drongo, but is a quiet bird. Returns to its perch after catching prey on the ground. (Suidelike swartvlieëvanger)

694

Fiscal Flycatcher

This pied flycatcher is distinguished from the similar Common Fiscal Shrike by its more slender bill, the white wingbar which is lower down on the wing and the white rectangles in the more rounded tail (seen in flight). The female is blackish brown where the male is black. Perches on top of a bush or tree from were it flies down to catch insects on the ground. Usually solitary or in pairs. (Fiskaalvlieëvanger)

698

Fairy Flycatcher

A very small, slender and attractive flycatcher. The black stripe through the eye, bordered with white, and the white wingbar and outer tail feathers are conspicuous. The immature is browner than the adult. Warbler-like in habits: forages within bushes or in the canopies of trees where it gleans insects off the branches. Often bobs and fans the tail, especially when breeding. (Feevlieëvanger)

706

Dusky Flycatcher
Similar to the Spotted Flycatcher, but smaller and darker. The crown and breast are indistinctly streaked. The white eye-ring is not always visible. The upperparts are greyer than those of the Spotted Flycatcher, while the latter's crown is streaked. Keeps to tall trees in forest, dense woodland, plantations and even gardens. Perches on a low branch. Catches insects in flight or on the ground. A quiet bird.
(Donkervlieëvanger)

690

Spotted Flycatcher
Differs from other similar flycatchers by its streaked underparts and crown. (The Dusky Flycatcher is smaller and darker, especially on the back.) Found in summer wherever there are trees. A quiet bird which most frequently perches on a low branch of a tree. From here it hawks insects in flight or on the ground, often returning to the same perch. Sits with its head drawn into the shoulders.
(Europese vlieëvanger)

689

Eurasia

Marico Flycatcher
The pure white underparts, contrasting with the brown upperparts, are diagnostic. (The Pallid Flycatcher has light yellow-brown underparts.) Similar to the Pallid Flycatcher in habits, but is confined to thornveld areas. Found in groups of three to five. Perches on the outer branch of a tree from where it flies to the ground to forage. Holds the tail up while hopping around.
(Maricovlieëvanger)

695

Chat Flycatcher

A large, brown chat-like flycatcher with lighter underparts. Best distinguished from other similar flycatchers by its distribution and habitat. Often seen perched on bushes, shrubs or even telephone wires in fairly open country. From there it drops heavily onto prey on the ground. Its movements are more sluggish than those of other flycatchers.
(Grootvlieëvanger)

697

African Paradise Flycatcher

The orange-brown upperparts and tail make this blue-grey bird highly conspicuous. The dark blue head is crested. The male has very long central tail feathers (not only in the breeding season). Inhabits dense vegetation, preferably areas with large trees or well-wooded gardens. Here it would be easily overlooked, were it not for its continuous activity and calling. The flight is fast and rocket-like. (Afrikaanse paradysvlieëvanger)

710

2

Red-billed Oxpecker

Their habit of clinging to game in search of parasites such as ticks makes oxpeckers unmistakable. The more common Red-billed Oxpecker has a red bill and conspicuous yellow eye wattles. (The rare Yellow-billed Oxpecker has a red tip to the yellow bill and a pale rump.) The call of both species is a sharp hiss. The use of pesticides to kill ticks has reduced their numbers dramatically.
(Rooibekrenostervoël)

772

 3

European Starling

This glossy green starling looks blackish at a distance. Is distinguished by its yellow bill and white spots on the plumage. It is less glossy and more spotted when not breeding. Cecil John Rhodes introduced the first European Starlings to Cape Town in 1899. Since then they have spread, but are always found in association with humans.
Bold, yet wary of people. Forages on the ground.
(Europese spreeu)

757

Indian Myna

The orange-yellow legs, bill and bare area around the eyes are diagnostic. The white tail tip and large white wing patches are conspicuous in flight. This starling was introduced to Durban towards the end of the previous century and has spread from there. It is aggressive and competes with indigenous birds, but is fortunately confined to human settlements. Forages on the ground.
(Indiese spreeu)

758

Wattled Starling

A generally pale bird with black tips to the wings and a pale rump (seen in flight). The breeding male has a characteristic black and yellow head with black wattles on the head and throat. The non-breeding male resembles the female. Although widely distributed, it is more common in arid areas. A nomadic bird: flocks arrive in areas with good food supply, but leave again soon. The nest is built with thin branches and twigs.
(Lelspreeu)

760

122

Red-winged Starling

A large glossy-black starling with dark eyes. The rufous wingtips are characteristic and conspicuous in flight. (The Pale-winged Starling has orange eyes.) The female has a grey head, but the immature is similar to the male. This well-known starling frequents cliffs where their nests are built. In urban areas it breeds on buildings. The pairs mate for life, but young and unmated birds gather in flocks.

(Rooivlerkspreeu)

769

Pale-winged Starling

Similar to the Red-winged Starling, but the wingtips are cream-white and the eyes are orange. (The Red-winged Starling has rufous wingtips and dark eyes.) The distribution of this western species overlaps slightly with the more eastern Red-winged Starling. The habits of the two species are very similar, but the call of the Pale-winged Starling is less melodious. Both forage in trees and on the ground.

(Bleekvlerkspreeu)

770

African Pied Starling

A large, dark brown starling with a white lower belly and undertail coverts. The pale eyes and orange gape are conspicuous. The immature has dark eyes and a white gape. Flocks are a common sight along roads and on farms in grassland areas. Forages mostly on the ground. Flocks sleep together in trees or reeds. Several helpers aid in rearing the young.

(Afrikaanse witgatspreeu)

759

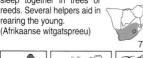

Glossy Starling

This is the most widespread of the glossy blue-green starlings with orange eyes. (The Greater Blue-eared Starling has a royal blue belly and dark blue ear patches.) It is found around trees in a variety of habitats, except in the eastern forests where it is replaced by the darker Black-bellied Starling. Forages in trees or on the ground, often visiting bird tables. It remains shy and wary.
(Kleinglansspreeu)

764

Greater Blue-eared Starling

The different species of glossy blue-green starling are best distinguished in good light. The Greater Blue-eared Starling has the most lustrous colour of them all. As the name indicates, the sides of the head are dark. The belly and flanks are royal blue. (The Lesser Blue-eared Starling has smaller ear patches and is confined to the miombo habitat.) Often more trusting than the Glossy Starling.
(Grootblouoorglansspreeu)

765

Black-bellied Starling

Very similar to the other glossy-blue starlings, but the plumage is duller and the eyes orange-yellow. The belly and flanks are black. Prefers a denser habitat than the two previous species. It inhabits the canopy of forest, coastal bush and dense riverine woodland where the exact colour is hard to distinguish. Forms pairs when breeding. Otherwise occurs in nomadic flocks. Very vocal.
(Swartpensglansspreeu)

768

Burchell's Starling

Distinguished from other glossy-blue starlings by its large size, dark eyes and the long broad tail with a rounded tip. (The similar Meve's Long-tailed Starling has a limited distribution and a very long tail which becomes thinner towards the tip.) Usually alone, in pairs or in small groups. A conspicuous bird which often perches on tree tops, but forages on the ground, especially in short grass. (Grootglansspreeu)

762

Meve's Long-tailed Starling

The dark eye distinguishes it from all glossy-blue starlings except the slightly larger Burchell's Starling. The tail is very long (longer than that of Burchell's Starling) and pointed, not round at the tip. It has a limited northerly distribution where it inhabits mopane and other woodland. Small groups sometimes gather to form large flocks. Forages on the ground, but flies strongly. (Mevese langstertglansspreeu)

763

Plum-coloured Starling

The male is unmistakable. The female may be distinguished from other similar birds, like the Groundscraper Thrush, by its yellow gape and eyes. The immature resembles the female, but has darker eyes. Non-breeding birds often congregate in flocks of the same sex. This fruit-eating starling is usually seen in trees. It breeds in holes in trees or even in pipes. (Witborsspreeu)

761

Southern Grey Tit

The different grey tits look very similar with their black heads and white band under the eye. The brownish appearance, especially the brown back, of the Southern Grey Tit is diagnostic. (The similar Northern Grey Tit occurs in Zimbabwe.) It frequents the shrubs of its Karoo habitat. Similar in habits to the next species. The Afrikaans name is an imitation of the call.
(Piet-tjou-tjou-grysmees)

551

Ashy Tit

Very similar to the Southern Grey Tit with a black head and throat and a white band under the eye, but is more greyish (not brown). The immature is duller than the adult. This is a tree-living species, preferring dry thornveld areas and Kalahari scrub. A restless bird which continuously hops from one branch to the next. Often hangs upside down while feeding. Acacia seed pods are torn open in search of insects. (Acaciagrysmees)

552

Southern Black Tit

A small black bird with white markings on the wings and under the tail. The belly is more grey, and the tip of the tail also shows white. The female is slightly greyer than the male. A noisy woodland species, chattering continuously to keep the small flock together. Sometimes joins other bird species when foraging. Feeds mostly on caterpillars which are often extracted from *Combretum* pods held down with the feet.
(Gewone swartmees)

554

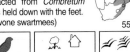

Group 11c: Insectivores with tiny bills

Not only their bills, but these birds themselves are tiny. This often makes it difficult to ascertain the shape of their bills. Just like those of the other insectivores, their bills have slightly decurved upper jaws.

The **penduline tits** are very small, with more pointed bills. They are active, gregarious birds. The conspicuous oval nest is built of felted plant and animal fibres. Below the true entrance, which closes, is a false entrance to mislead predators.

White-eyes are well-known garden birds, characterized by their yellowish colour and white eye-rings. They not only feed on insects, but also eat soft fruit and drink nectar.

The **warblers** and related **apalises, crombecs, eremomelas, cisticolas** and **prinias** are often difficult to identify as many of them lack striking colour patterns. Their habits, habitats and calls should therefore also be noted for positive identification. Most are fairly shy, foraging for insects under the cover of vegetation.

Cape Penduline Tit

The forehead of this very small bird is black with small white spots. A black line runs through the eye and the underparts are yellow. Small groups forage restlessly for insects among the branches of trees and bushes. (The Grey Penduline Tit has an easterly distribution. It is buffy below, light grey on the breast, white on the face and throat and lacks the Cape Penduline Tit's forehead pattern.)
(Kaapse kapokvoël)

557

| | | Unique 5 |

Cape White-eye

A very small greenish-yellow bird with a conspicuous white eye-ring. The back is grey-green, while the colour of the underparts varies according to the different parts of its distribution (a and b). (The Yellow White-eye is more greenish with a yellow belly and occurs in the north-east.) Groups actively forage for insects in trees and bushes. Also feeds on nectar by piercing the base of a flower.
(Kaapse glasogie)

796

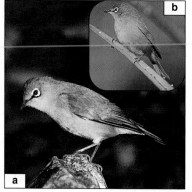

| | | 3 |

Chestnut-vented Tit-babbler

The chestnut-brown feathers under the tail are the best field characteristic. The eyes are white, and the throat and breast boldly streaked (more than those of Layard's Tit-babbler, which is white under the tail). The Afrikaans name imitates its call "cherik-tiktik", which is often heard. A tame and restless bird, but it usually remains hidden in the canopy of a tree, gleaning insects off branches. (Bosveldtjeriktik)

621

Bar-throated Apalis

The amount of yellow on the belly and green on the back varies between birds from different parts of the distribution area. The pale eye and the black band across the breast (less pronounced in the female) are distinctive. The white outer tail feathers can be seen in flight. (Rudd's Apalis has a dark eye and no white outer tail feathers.) Although quite tame, it keeps to the cover of vegetation. (Bandkeelkleinjantjie)

645

Yellow-breasted Apalis

The black band below the characteristic yellow breast may be absent or present. The throat and belly are white, while the amount of grey on the head varies between individuals. Forages actively for insects in the canopy of trees or in bushes in moist bushveld, riverine bush or other thickets, normally keeping to cover. Like the Bar-throated Apalis it is often seen in the company of other bird species. (Geelborskleinjantjie)

648

Yellow-bellied Eremomela

The upperparts are olive-grey, the breast and throat pale grey, the belly yellow. Similar to the Cape Penduline Tit, but has a dark line through the eye. This very small bird is found in a wide variety of habitats, from arid scrub to woodland. Single birds or pairs move actively through the foliage of smaller trees and bushes. Often joins other birds while foraging for small insects. A tame but unobtrusive bird.
(Geelpensbossanger)

653

Willow Warbler

This very small bird could be mistaken for a Garden Warbler, but has a clear white eyebrow and a slightly notched tail tip. The throat and breast are washed with yellow. (The Icterine Warbler has pale yellow underparts and a larger bill.) This is the most common and widely distributed of the migrant warblers visiting southern Africa. It forages for small insects within the canopy of a tree or bush.
(Hofsanger)

643

North. hemisph.

Green-backed Bleating Warbler

The bleating alarm call identifies this small warbler. Its back is olive-yellow, the underparts greyish. (The Karoo Eremomela has white underparts. The Grey-backed Bleating Warbler has a grey back and occurs further north.) Hops around the lower branches of thickets, the tail characteristically cocked. The male displays by jumping up and down on its perch.
(Groenkwê-kwêvoël)

657a

Great Reed Warbler

This warbler is best identified by its large size (like a bulbul), and its harsh warbling song. It has a brown back and pale eyebrows. The song, difficult to describe, consists of a series of grating "kurk-kurk" and creaking "twee-tweet" sounds. Found not only among reeds, but also in thickets and even in gardens. It flies low from cover to cover, spreading its tail in flight.
(Grootrietsanger)

628

Eurasia

Cape Reed Warbler

Once one is familiar with the song, a series of melodious warbling and bubbling sounds, this is one of the easiest warblers to identify. The body is brown on the back with white underparts and a conspicuous white eyebrow. (Larger than the European and African Marsh Warblers.) Always associated with beds of reeds and other similar vegetation. Although it is very inquisitive, it keeps to cover.
(Kaapse rietsanger)

635

2

African Sedge Warbler

Its dark brown colour, spotted breast and throat, and broad, rounded tail are distinctive. This warbler is less often seen than other warblers, as it prefers the densest growth of reeds and rushes. Here it creeps about like a mouse, keeping just above the water level. Its distinctive call, however, is often heard: sounding like a stick drawn across the spokes of a bicycle wheel.
(Kaapse vleisanger)

638

2

Fan-tailed Cisticola

Cisticolas are very small, similarly coloured birds, best identified by their habitat, call and habits. This cisticola is very widely distributed. The monotonous "zit zit zit zit", given at one-second intervals, attracts attention to the displaying male while he flies at a height of up to 15 m above grassland or fallow lands.
The nest looks like a bottle of plant material.
(Landeryklopkloppie)

664

Unique
3

Rattling Cisticola

This is the most conspicuous and common cisticola in thornveld and dry woodland, especially during summer when the male displays. It perches on the top of a tree while singing its characteristic song. This starts with a "cheer cheer cheer", followed by a series of rattling calls. The female is shy, keeping closer to the ground. (The similar Tinkling Cisticola has a darker spotted back and a rufous tail.)
(Bosveldtinktinkie)

672

3

Le Vaillant's Cisticola

The red (not grey) tail distinguishes it from the similar Black-backed Cisticola. Never found far from water, this cisticola frequents vleis, marshy areas and moist grassland along streams and dams. It is conspicuous, perching on tall plants when disturbed and uttering the "dzwee dzwee dzwee" alarm call. The song starts with one or more soft "tsee" calls, followed by a series of bubbling notes.
(Vleitinktinkie)

677

 4

Neddicky

This plain-coloured grey-brown cisticola is frequently seen in trees and bushes. Southern birds are more greyish (b). It wags its short tail sideways. (The Lazy Cisticola has a longer tail.) It occurs in open woodland with grass cover, or on mountain sides in the south. The song is a monotonous "teep teep". The distinctive alarm call sounds like a finger run across the teeth of a comb. (Neddikkie)

681

3

Long-billed Crombec

Crombecs are very small birds with extremely short tails (they look tailless). The widely distributed Long-billed Crombec has a white eyebrow and a dark line through the eye, while the similar Red-faced Crombec is confined to Zimbabwe and Mozambique. Crombecs are restless birds, often joining other birds while searching the foliage of trees and bushes for insects. They usually start low down and work their way up. (Bosveldstompstert)

651

2

Tawny-flanked Prinia

Prinias are very small brown birds, the long tails often held cocked upwards. The Tawny-flanked Prinia is the common prinia in the moister eastern parts of southern Africa. The back is grey-brown and the underparts are white with tawny flanks. It occurs in a variety of habitats, frequenting the middle and lower strata of trees and bushes. Tame and trusting. (Bruinsylangstertjie)

683

3

Black-chested Prinia

The black breastband is conspicuous during the breeding season, but absent or indistinct in winter, when the underparts are more yellow and contrast with the white throat. This is a widely distributed prinia in the thornveld of the dry west, often coming into gardens. Like other prinias, it perches conspicuously when disturbed, while uttering its sharp alarm call.
(Swartbandlangstertjie)

685

3

Nbr | Br

Karoo Prinia

The yellowish underparts, spotted with dark markings, are diagnostic. The eyebrows, face and throat are white. Found in arid habitat types. (The very similar Drakensberg Prinia prefers moister habitats. The Namaqua Prinia has white underparts with rufous flanks and is found under thorntrees along rivers.) Usually keeps to cover, but perches conspicuously when disturbed.
(Karoolangstertjie)

686a

4

Rufous-eared Warbler

This prinia-like warbler has a characteristic black breastband and rufous ear patches. The ear patches of the male are brighter and the breastband bolder than in females. It favours the low scrub habitats of the arid western areas. Forages on the ground with the tail cocked upwards. When alarmed it runs or flies low towards the closest cover. The male sings from the top of a bush.
(Rooioorsanger)

688

 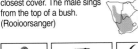

4

Group 12: Seedeaters

Doves and the larger **pigeons** require no introduction. They swallow seeds whole, often feeding on larger seeds than other seedeaters.

Most seedeaters (many of which are known as finches) are small birds with stout, conical bills. **Sparrows**, some well-known garden birds, are mostly brown in colour. Many male **weavers** are predominantly yellow. The females and non-breeding males are duller and more difficult to identify. Their nests are intricately woven. **Firefinches** are very small, reddish seedeaters. They are similar to the **waxbills**, a group of very small but brightly coloured birds. The bishops and widows are closely related as shown by their similar females and non-breeding males. Male **bishops** are boldly coloured in black and red or yellow. Male **widows** are mostly black. **Whydahs** are characterized by their long tails, while the **widowfinches** are glossy black. Both are nesting parasites. Female and non-breeding male whydahs have striped heads, but not as boldly striped as those of the **buntings**. Many, but not all, **canaries** are yellow.

African Green Pigeon

A large green pigeon vaguely resembling a parrot. The leg feathers are yellow, the legs and the base of the bill are red. The heads and underparts of birds from different parts of the distribution area differ from grey-green to yellow-green. Inhabits dense woodland and riverine bush, up to the edge of evergreen forests. Forages in fruit-bearing trees: often feeds on figs. Well camouflaged.
(Papegaaiduif)

361

Namaqua Dove

A small dove with a characteristically long, pointed tail. The male has a black face and an orange-yellow bill with a purple base. The immature is mottled. In flight the rufous flight feathers and bands across the back are conspicuous, but it is distinguished from the Green-spotted Dove by its long tail. Found in thornbush and grassland – even in arid areas. Forages on open patches.
(Namakwaduifie)

356

Rameron Pigeon

A large, dark, purple-brown pigeon, spotted with white. The yellow bill and toes are characteristic. The head is grey, the bare facial ring yellow. (The Rock Pigeon is more maroon-brown and the bare facial skin is red. The Feral Pigeon is mostly grey with a metallic green neck.) Shy. Frequents the canopy of forests and plantations. Sometimes forages far afield. Seldom comes down to the ground. (Geelbekbosduif)

350

Rock Pigeon

The neck, back and wings are maroon-brown, the wings spotted with white. The underparts and head are grey and there is a characteristic bare red area around the yellow eyes. (The Feral Pigeon has a metallic green neck and the Rameron Pigeon a yellow bill and toes.) Found on cliffs, rocky hills, in kloofs and on buildings, where they roost and breed. The male has a clapping display flight. Forages on farmlands. (Kransduif)

349

Feral Pigeon

The well-known pigeon found in cities and towns. Various colour variations exist (a and b), the most common being grey with metallic green patches on the sides of the neck. Introduced to southern Africa from Europe for mail and racing. Forages in huge flocks on streets and city squares. The male claps its wings during the courtship flight. Breeds on ledges of buildings. (Tuinduif)

348

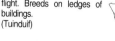

Red-eyed Dove

The largest of the doves with a half-collar on the back of the neck. The underparts are more pink than those of other collared doves. The cap is grey. The eye and the bare eye-ring are deep red. The tail lacks any white feathers. The call sounds like "I am – a Red-eyed Dove". Found in well-developed bush-veld, riverine bush and gardens with large trees. Forages on the ground. More wary than other doves. (Grootringduif)

352

African Mourning Dove

The bare red ring around the yellow eyes, the grey head and the pale pink underparts are characteristic. The tips of the outer tail feathers are white. (The Red-eyed Dove is larger and darker with red eyes. The Cape Turtle Dove has black eyes.) Occurs in dry riverine bush, rural villages and rest camps in game reserves. Tame. Forages on the ground. The call is a soft "krrrow-rrrrr". (Rooioogtortelduif)

353

Cape Turtle Dove

A pale grey turtle dove with black eyes. In flight the white outer tail feathers are visible. Is often confused with the Red-eyed Dove, which is larger, has pinkish underparts and red eyes. Widely distributed; occurs in woodland, bushveld, riverine bush and gardens, even in very arid regions. Forages on the ground, but roosts in trees. Tame and confiding in urban areas. The call is the well-known "work harr-der". (Gewone tortelduif)

354

Laughing Dove

The reddish breast is characteristically speckled black. Similar to the turtle doves, but lacks the half-collar on the back of the neck. In flight the white outer tail feathers are visible. Widespread; found in open woodland and arid bushveld, but absent from very arid country where Cape Turtle Doves still occur. Quickly establishes itself in gardens. Forages on the ground. The call sounds like someone laughing.
(Rooiborsduifie)

355

Green-spotted Dove

A smallish dove with green iridescent spots on the wings. The rufous wingtips and bands across the back are visible in flight. Occurs in most types of bushveld. (The Blue-spotted Dove prefers denser vegetation, and has a limited distribution. The tip of its bill is yellow.) The call is a series of melancholic "du du du du" sounds, starting slowly and then speeding up. Forages on the ground and has a very quick take-off or landing. (Groenvlekduifie)

358

Tambourine Dove

The white face and underparts are diagnostic. The female and the immature have grey throats and breasts. The eyebrows of the male are conspicuous. The orange-brown underwing is seen in flight. The call is similar to that of the Green-spotted Dove, but it ends abruptly. Found in dense vegetation like evergreen forests and dense bushveld. Forages in open patches in woodland or on roads.
(Witborsduifie)

359

White-browed Sparrow-weaver

Identified by the broad white eyebrow, and the white rump and underparts. The north-eastern population has brown spots on the breast (b). (Sociable Weavers lack the white eyebrows and have black chevron marks on the flanks.) Very noisy. Inhabits thorn and mopane veld. A number of birds build their nests in the same tree. Some of these nests are used for roosting at night. Forages on the ground in the vicinity of the nesting site. (Koringvoël)

799

Sociable Weaver

A pale sparrow-like bird. The pale blue bill, black facial mask and black chevron markings on the flanks are characteristic. The habitat is arid thornveld and semi-desert with quiver trees. Colonies breed in the well-known giant nests, which are built in trees or on telephone poles. On the underside of the nest are the chambers in which pairs roost and breed. Noisy at the nest. (Versamelvoël)

800

Unique
4

Scaly-feathered Finch

A small sparrow-like bird which is identified by its pink bill and black moustachial stripes. The tail feathers and the feathers on the wings appear scaled as each feather has a white edge. The forehead is black and white. Inhabits arid scrub, thornveld and the vegetation along dry river courses. Forages on the ground, but flies to the nearest cover when alarmed. Small groups roost in special nests or close together on a branch. Tame. (Baardmannetjie)

806

House Sparrow

Common around human habitation. Its grey cap and black bib on the breast identify the male. (The similar Great Sparrow is a veld bird.) The female and the immature have pinkish bills and dull eyebrows. The grey rump distinguishes it from other indigenous sparrows. Originates from Europe and India. Always near humans. Forages on the ground. Becomes fairly tame, but remains wary.
(Huismossie)

801

Cape Sparrow

The male has a black head and breast; the white eyebrow forms a large "C" on the side of the head. The female is paler; the "C" on her grey head is not as bold, but distinguishes her from other sparrows, such as Southern Grey-headed Sparrow. Found in gardens and in a variety of more arid habitats, often near water. The nests are untidy balls of grass and other material. Special nests are built to roost in.
(Gewone mossie)

803

4

Southern Grey-headed Sparrow

The completely grey head and the short white wingbar are characteristic. (The females of other sparrows have pale or light yellow eyebrows or other markings on the grey head.) Forages on the ground on open bare patches in arid bush and thornveld. Is often seen around farmhouses. Usually in flocks, but pairs breed in holes in trees or walls and other cavities.
(Suidelike gryskopmossie)

804

3

Red-billed Buffalo Weaver

Large, noisy black weavers with diagnostic orange-red bills and white wing patches, visible in flight. The female is browner with mottled underparts. The immature has a dark bill. Found in arid bushveld around large trees such as camelthorns and baobabs. Flocks feed on the ground, often in association with starlings. Roosts communally in the central chambers of the nests: large untidy structures built of thorny twigs.   (Buffelwewer)

798

3

Red-headed Weaver

The head, neck and back of the male in his breeding plumage are bright red; those of the female and non-breeding male are yellow. Both sexes have orange bills and white underparts. Inhabits various types of bushveld, usually near water. A quiet bird which is easily overlooked. The untidy nest is built of twigs and coarse plant material. It has a long spout.
(Rooikopwewer)

819

3

Red-billed Quelea

Non-breeding males and females are dull birds with red legs and bills. The bill of the breeding female is yellow. The breeding male has a red bill and a black facial mask which may be edged with red or yellow. Found in grassy country. Huge flocks fly in a well co-ordinated way. Breeds in colonies, usually in thorn trees. May become an agricultural problem, especially in wheat-producing areas.
(Rooibekkwelea)

821

3

Thick-billed Weaver

The large bill and white patches on the forehead are characteristic. The male is dark brown. The white wing patches are visible in flight. The female is light brown with boldly spotted underparts. (The female Plum-coloured Starling has a thinner bill and a streaked back.) Breeds in reed beds. Forages in the canopy of forest, up to 30 km away from the nests and even in gardens. The nest is neatly woven between two reeds. (Dikbekwewer) 807

Spectacled Weaver

The prominent black eyestripe and pale yellow eyes distinguish it from all yellow weavers. The face is orange. The male has a black throat and the female's is golden-yellow. Found in riverine bush and other thickets up to the forest edge; also in gardens. Forages for insects among the foliage of trees and shrubs. Calls continuously, but is difficult to see. The woven nest has a long entrance spout. (Brilwewer) 810

Cape Weaver

The breeding male is distinguished from other yellow weavers by its yellow eyes and orange-brown face. The female and non-breeding male have olive-brown backs and buff underparts. The large size (this is our largest weaver) and long pointed bill aid identification. Usually in groups. Found in open woodland and riverine vegetation, reed beds and even gardens usually near water. Aggressive. (Kaapse wewer) 813

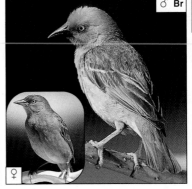

Spotted-backed Weaver

The breeding male has a spotted back, a black facial mask and a yellow forehead. (The black mask of the Southern and Lesser Masked Weavers extends onto the forehead.) The northern population has a totally black head (b). The female and non-breeding male have white bellies and grey-brown backs. Found in bushveld and coastal areas near water. Breeds in colonies, often in reeds or a large tree overhanging water. (Bontrugwewer)

811

Southern Masked Weaver

The breeding male is distinguished from the male Spotted-backed Weaver by its uniformly coloured back and black facial mask extending onto the forehead. (The Lesser Masked Weaver has pale eyes and a larger black facial mask.) Found commonly in various habitats usually near water. Breeds in colonies. A male has more than one female and destroys the nest if the female does not approve of it. (Swartkeelgeelvink)

814

Lesser Masked Weaver

The breeding male's mask extends to behind the eye. The pale eye distinguishes it from the Spotted-backed and Southern Masked Weavers. The female is yellower than females of the other two black-faced weaver species. A bushveld bird, usually breeds in large trees near water. Forages in the canopy of trees. Usually breeds in small colonies, often with the previous two species. (Kleingeelvink)

815

Black-cheeked Waxbill

A deep red-brown waxbill. The black cheeks and dark bill are characteristic. The crown, neck and back are greyer, the wings are finely barred black. The female resembles the male, but is paler on the breast and flanks. Is usually associated with arid bushveld, especially thornveld and riverine thickets in this habitat. Forages (usually in small groups) on the ground near cover. Roosts in nests.
(Swartwangsysie)

847

Violet-eared Waxbill

A colourful waxbill with a long tail, blue forehead and rump, and characteristic violet ear patches in the male and pale blue ear patches in the female. The male's underparts are chestnut, its throat black. The female is paler with light brown underparts. Found in arid bushveld, especially thornveld with thickets and riverine bush. Forages on the ground, often near water-holes. Brood host of the Shaft-tailed Whydah.
(Koningblousysie)

845

Blue Waxbill

Identified by the blue face, breast and flanks. The crown, back and wings are brown. The female is paler than the male. The immature is even paler than the female with a dark bill. Found along rivers and in open thornveld with patches of grass, shrubs and bare areas. Small flocks forage on the ground, often mixing with other seed-eaters. When disturbed, it flies into the nearest tree.
(Gewone blousysie)

844

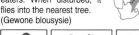

Blue-billed Firefinch

Very similar to Jameson's Firefinch which also has a blue bill. The upperparts and wings, however, are darker brown. It prefers the edges of forests, riverine bush and thickets. (Jameson's Firefich, with a pinkish back, inhabits open bushveld. The Red-billed Firefinch has a red bill.) The male has a dark belly. Forages on the ground or low in shrubs. Brood host of the Black Widow-finch. (Kaapse vuurvinkie)

840

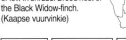

4

Red-billed Firefinch

The red bill distinguishes both sexes from the Blue-billed and Jameson's Firefinches which have blue bills. The female is brown. Its red rump distinguishes it from the Brown Firefinch which occurs in the Okavango. Inhabits thickets with grass, especially on open patches in thornveld where it forages. Like other firefinches it is easily overlooked. Brood host of the Steel-blue Widow-finch. (Rooibekvuurvinkie)

842

3

Common Waxbill

A pale grey-brown waxbill identified by its red bill and red band through the eye. The central belly is pale red, the undertail is black. At close range the body is barred dark. The immature lacks the red bill and eyestripe. Found in grass, reeds and other rank vegetation near water. Forages on the ground. Flocks roost in reed beds. Very active. Brood host of the Pin-tailed Whydah. (Rooibeksysie)

846

5

Melba Finch

Both sexes have characteristically banded underparts and red bills. The male's face and throat are bright red, which is absent in the female. (The Golden-backed Pytilia, in Zimbabwe, has orange wings. Its underparts are not as boldly barred.) Found in grassy patches on the edge of riverine bush or other thickets in dense grass. Forages on the ground in open patches. Brood host of the Paradise Whydah.
(Gewone melba)

834

Quail Finch

A very small waxbill which is more often heard than seen. The call sounds like tiny bells. Both sexes have red bills, white eye-rings and characteristically barred breasts and flanks. The male has a dark face and a black throatband. Found in open, short grassland with bare patches, near marshes and pans or on Kalahari sand. Forages on the ground. Flushes at the last moment when approached.
(Gewone kwartelvinkie)

852

Orange-breasted Waxbill

The orange-yellow underparts are diagnostic of this waxbill. Both sexes have red bills and rumps. The flanks are finely barred. The male has red eyestripes and an orange patch on the breast, features which are absent in the female. Found in grassland or bushveld with long rank grass, usually near water. Forages on the ground or among grass. May build its own nest, but usually breeds in the old nests of Southern Red Bishops.   (Rooiassie)

854

Cut-throat Finch

The male's red band across the throat is diagnostic. The female resembles the male, but lacks this red band. The heads of both sexes are finely barred. (The female Red-headed Finch has a plain brown head and neck.) Found in arid bushveld. A quiet bird that forages on the ground. Can build its own nests, but also roosts and breeds in old weaver nests or in natural cavities.
(Bandkeelvink)

855

Red-headed Finch

The male's red head is characteristic; the female has a grey-brown head. Both sexes have grey-brown backs. Their underparts are spotted with white, each spot edged black; the female's spots are duller. Inhabits farmlands and grassy patches in arid bushveld. Forages on the ground. Drinks regularly. Breeds during winter in pairs or small colonies. Uses old nests of weavers and sparrows or natural cavities.   (Rooikopvink)

856

Southern Red Bishop

The male's bright red and black breeding plumage is very conspicuous. The black on its face covers the forehead. (The Fire-crowned Bishop occurs in a small area in the north-east. It has a red crown.) The female and non-breeding male resemble Golden Bishops, but have more boldly striped breasts. Frequents rank grass or reed beds. One male may have up to seven females.
(Suidelike rooivink)

824

Golden Bishop

The breeding male's bright yellow back and crown are conspicuous. The underparts are black. The female and non-breeding male resemble those of the Red Bishop, but their bellies are paler and the backs slightly rufous. Found in rank grass, in reed beds on marshes or near dams. Forages on grass stems or on the ground. When displaying, the male resembles a bumble bee in flight.
(Goudgeelvink)

826

Yellow-rumped Widow

The yellow rump distinguishes the breeding male from other short-tailed widows. (The White-winged Widow has a white shoulder patch. The Yellow-backed Widow lacks the yellow rump and has a long tail.) The female has a dull yellow rump and streaked breast. Non-breeding males resemble females, but the shoulders and rump are yellow. Found in rank grass and marshes, on slopes or in valleys. A male may have up to three females.   (Kaapse flap)

827

♂ Br

White-winged Widow

The breeding male is black with white and yellow patches on the wing, and a blue-grey bill. The male displays by fanning its tail. The non-breeding male resembles the female, but is larger and retains the coloured wing patches. (The non-breeding Yellow-rumped Widow retains its yellow rump.) Found in rank grassland next to farmlands and roads, usually in thornveld. A male may have up to four females.
(Witvlerkflap)

829

147

♂ Br

Red-shouldered Widow
The breeding male is the only short-tailed widow with red shoulders. The non-breeding male and female resemble each other, but the female is smaller and has golden brown shoulders while the male's shoulders are rufous. (The non-breeding Long-tailed Widow is similar, but larger.) Found in marshes and open rank grassland. Forages mostly on the ground. A male has more than one female. (Kortstertflap)

828

3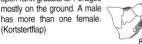

♂ Br ♀

Long-tailed Widow
The black breeding male has characteristic red shoulders with a buff area underneath. The tail is longer and thicker than that of the Red-collared Widow. The shoulder patches are paler in the brown non-breeding male. The female is smaller and lacks the red shoulder patches. Inhabits open grassland, marshes and valleys, especially in moist country. Flocks roost in reed beds. A male may have up to six females. (Langstertflap)

832

3

♂ Br

Red-collared Widow
The long tail and red band across the throat distinguish the black breeding male. (The Long-tailed Widow has a red and buff shoulder patch and no red band across the throat.) The female is similar to the non-breeding male, with plain underparts and lacking the shoulder patches. Found in rank grass in marshes, valleys and open bushveld. Forages on the ground or on grasses. A male may have up to three females. (Rooikeelflap)

831

3

Paradise Whydah

The breeding male has a very distinctive plumage and long tail. (The Broad-tailed Paradise Whydah has a broader tail tip and is found in the north-east; non-breeding males are similar.) The female and non-breeding male have grey bills and paler head bands and bellies than the Pin-tailed Whydah. Prefers thornveld. The breeding male hovers with an undulating tail. Brood parasitises Melba Finches.
(Gewone paradysvink)

862

Breeding parasite

 ♂ Br
 ♀

Pin-tailed Whydah

The breeding male's long tail feathers and white underparts (yellow in the Shaft-tailed Whydah) are characteristic. The bill remains red when not breeding. The female and non-breeding male have more boldly striped heads than the Shaft-tailed Whydah, and their legs are grey. Found in open bushveld and grassland. Forages on the ground and chases other birds. Brood parasitises main-ly the Common Waxbill.
(Koningrooibekkie)

860

Breeding parasite

 ♂ Nbr
♂ Br

Shaft-tailed Whydah

The breeding male's underparts are tawny yellow. The long spatula-shaped tail feathers differ from those of the Pin-tailed Whydah. The bill remains orange-red when not breeding. The non-breeding male (similar to the female) has a less distinctively striped head than the other whydahs. The legs are dull red. Found in arid thornveld. Forages on the ground. Brood parasitises the Violet-eared Waxbill. The male has more than one female.
(Pylstertrooibekkie)

861

Breeding parasite

 ♀
 ♂ Br

149

♂ Br

Steel-blue Widow-finch

Both sexes have red legs and bills. (The Purple Widow-finch has a white bill and pinkish legs. The Black Widow-finch has a white bill and red legs.) The breeding male is black. The female and non-breeding male are brown with boldly striped heads. Inhabits arid bushveld and thickets with rank grass. Forages on bare patches on the ground. Brood parasitises the Red-billed Firefinch. (Staalblouvinkie)

867

		Breeding parasite

♂ Br

Purple Widow-finch

The white bills and pale legs distinguish both sexes from other widow-finches. (The Steel-blue Widow-finch has a red bill and legs. The Black Widow-finch has a white bill and red legs.) The breeding male is black. The female and non-breeding male are brown with boldly striped heads. Found in arid thornveld, bush-veld and farmland. Forages on the ground. Brood parasitises Jameson's Firefinch. (Witpootblouvinkie)

865

		Breeding parasite

Bronze Mannikin

The brown back, black head and white underparts, finely barred on the flanks, are characteristic. The upper jaw is black, the lower grey. (The Red-backed Mannikin, an eastern species, has a black head, neck and breast, a rufous back and a grey bill.) The immature is plain buff. Found in grassy areas in moist bushveld near thickets and on old farmlands. Small flocks forage on the ground or on grasses. Roosts in nests. (Gewone fret)

857

		5

Golden-breasted Bunting

Identified by the striped head, the golden breast and rufous back. There is a white band above and below the eyes. (Cabanis's Bunting, in the north-east, has a grey back and black cheeks without the white band below the eye.) Found in various types of woodland and bushveld, as well as in riverine bush. Forages on the ground among grass and shrubs, not in the open. When disturbed, it flies into a tree.
(Rooirugstreepkoppie)

884

Cape Bunting

The grey back and breast and rufous wings distinguish it from other buntings. The throat and the bands above and below the eyes are white. (The Cinnamon-breasted Rock Bunting has a black throat and a cinnamon-coloured body.) Usually found in rocky areas, even in arid country, but often near water. Forages on the ground. Frequently calls from a rock. Although tame, it is easily overlooked.
(Rooivlerkstreepkoppie)

885

Cinnamon-breasted Rock Bunting

The cinnamon body and the male's boldly striped head and neck are characteristic. The heads of the female and immature are grey. (The Cape Bunting has a white throat and grey breast.) Found in rocky country: rocky hills, cliffs and dry river courses. When disturbed, it flies onto a rock which is used as a vantage point. Forages on the ground. An unobtrusive bird.
(Kaneelborsklipstreepkoppie)

886

151

Lark-like Bunting

A drab-looking bird that is difficult to identify. A pale, light cinnamon bird resembling a lark. The wings are darker (buff-rufous) than the underparts. The eyebrow and moustachial stripes are buff-white. Prefers arid country: rocky hills or mountain slopes and dry river courses, but is usually near water. Always nomadic. Often calls from a rock or the top of a shrub. (Vaalstreepkoppie)

887

Black-throated Canary

The finely streaked head and the black-speckled throat are diagnostic. The yellow rump contrasts with the pale brown body. The white-tipped tail is visible in flight. (The larger White-throated Canary also has a yellow rump, but the bill is larger and the throat white.) Inhabits arid woodland, bushveld and riverine vegetation, usually near water. Groups forage mostly on the ground, but also in trees, grass and shrubs. Unobtrusive. (Bergkanarie)

870

White-throated Canary

The white throat, very large bill and yellow rump are diagnostic. (The Black-throated Canary, also with a yellow rump, has a black-speckled throat. Streaky-headed and Protea Canaries, with white throats, lack the yellow rump.) The habitat is arid thornveld, Karoo scrub, coastal bush and desert, usually near water. Drinks regularly. Forages mostly on the ground, but also in shrubs. Nomadic. A quiet bird. (Witkeelkanarie)

879

152

Cape Canary

The grey nape and sides of the neck are characteristic. The yellow forehead and crown further distinguish this canary from other yellow canaries. The female is paler than the male, the grey nape extending around the neck, meeting on the breast. Found in hilly scrub, montane grassland and cultivated fields. Forages on the ground or on grass stems. Sometimes breeds in colonies.
(Kaapse kanarie)

872

Yellow-eyed Canary

Very similar to the Yellow Canary, but occurs in various types of bushveld, woodland and riverine bush. The characteristic facial pattern consists of conspicuous black eye and moustachial stripes. The crown and neck are grey. (Bully Canaries are larger with larger bills and the facial pattern is less prominent.) Forages mostly on the ground. Flies into the nearest tree when disturbed.
(Geeloogkanarie)

869

Yellow Canary

Similar to the Yellow-eyed Canary, but occurs in the arid west. The facial pattern is less prominent than in the Yellow-eyed Canary. The male becomes progressively darker on the upperparts towards the north-east. (The Bully Canary is brighter and has a larger bill.) The female is greyer, her underparts streaked. Found in various types of scrub and grassland, even in very arid country.
(Geelkanarie)

878

153

Abbreviated alphabetical index

Acknowledgements

Firstly, we would like to thank J.L. van Schaik Publishers for the trust they showed in us by publishing this book.

We would like to thank family and friends for the advice and sound ideas they contributed at the design stage.

To all wildlife photographers and agencies who kindly made slides available for this book – our special thanks. Without your contribution it would not have been possible.

Our sincere thanks to Anneliese for her outstanding illustrations drawn specially for this book.

Our thanks also to the Creator for the privilege of sharing a small part of our wonderful world with other people.

Burger and Ulrich

Bibliography

Brown, L.H., Urban, E.K. & Newman, K.B. (eds). 1982. **The Birds of Africa**, Vol. 1. Academic Press, London.

Fry, C.H., Keith, S. & Urban, E.K. (eds). 1988. **The Birds of Africa**, Vol. 3. Academic Press, London.

Ginn, P.J., McIlleron, W.G. & Milstein, P. le S. 1989. **The Complete Book of Southern African Birds**. Struik Winchester, Cape Town.

Harrison, J.A., Allen, D.G., Underhill, L.G., Herremans, M., Tree, A.J., Parker, V. & Brown, C.J. (eds). 1997. **The Atlas of Southern African Birds**, Vol. 1 & 2. BirdLife South Africa, Johannesburg.

Keith, S. Urban, E.K. & Fry, C.H. 1992. **The Birds of Africa**, Vol. 4. Academic Press, London.

Maclean, G.L. 1993. **Roberts' Birds of Southern Africa**. John Voelcker Bird Book Fund, Cape Town.

Newman, K. 1983. **Newman's Birds of Southern Africa**. Southern Book Publishers, Halfway House.

Sinclair, I., Hockey, P. & Tarboton, W. 1997. **Sasol Birds of Southern Africa**. Struik, Cape Town.

Sinclair, I. & Davidson, I. 1995. **Southern African Birds; a photographic guide**. Struik, Cape Town.

Sinclair, J.C. 1987. **Field Guide to the Birds of Southern Africa**. Struik, Cape Town.

Steyn, P. 1982. **Birds of Prey of Southern Africa**. David Philip, Cape Town.

Urban, E.K., Fry, C.H. & Keith, S. (eds). 1986. **The Birds of Africa**, Vol. 2. Academic Press, London.

Urban, E.K., Fry, C.H. & Keith, S. (eds). 1997. **The Birds of Africa,** Vol. 5. Academic Press, London.

Photographic credits

(In the case of two photographs, the main photo is always "a" and the other one "b")

ABPL/Thomas Dressler 583a, ABPL/Clem Haagner 153, ABPL/Beverley Joubert 154, ABPL/Brendon Ryan 740a, ABPL/Nigel Dennis 792a, ABPL/Peter Chadwick 163b, ABPL/Hein von Hörsten 483b, Daryl Balfour 96, 462, R M Bloomfield 489, 653, Cobie Botha 581a, 798a, Willem Botha 429b, 710b, Terry Carew 125b, 240a, 300, 344a, 395, 445, 494a, 697, 716, Burger Cillié 1a, 1b, 8b, 55a, 55b, 58a, 58b, 60b, 62, 63a, 64, 65b, 66a, 66b, 69a, 69b, 74a, 76b, 83, 87, 88a, 88b, 89, 90a, 93b, 99a, 99b, 100, 102, 106, 114b, 116b, 118, 123a, 126b, 146b, 148b, 188a, 189, 191, 196, 198b, 199, 203a, 208, 209, 223, 230, 237a, 237b, 246b, 255, 286, 295, 345a, 347a, 348b, 353, 354, 355, 356b, 361, 380, 382, 386a, 386b, 391, 405, 426, 428a, 428b, 435a, 440, 443, 444a, 444b, 446, 455, 459, 461, 463a, 463b, 464, 465, 473, 476, 486a, 487a, 487b, 494b, 495a , 495b, 496a, 496b, 498a, 500a, 506a, 507, 515b, 520, 522, 527, 538b, 541, 545a, 560, 563, 567, 568, 576, 577a, 580, 586a, 586c, 587b, 589, 593a, 595a, 595b, 599, 601, 613, 628, 664, 672, 681a, 685b, 694, 695, 703a, 717, 727, 728, 731, 732b, 733a, 733b, 736, 740b, 743, 753, 758, 759, 760a, 761b, 762, 764, 765, 769b, 775b, 787a, 787b, 788a, 791a, 791b, 792b, 793b, 796b, 798b, 799a, 800, 801a, 801b, 803a, 803b, 804, 806, 814b, 815a, 815b, 819a, 819b, 824b, 828, 829a, 832b, 842b, 854b, 855a, 856a, 860a, 860b, 861a, 861b, 862b, 865, 867a, 867b, 870, Andrew Deacon 93a, 140a, 297, 449, Roger de la Harpe 152a, 582b, Koos Delport 53a, 53b, 122a, 181, 344b, 581b, Nigel Dennis 6, 135a, 247, 474a, 635, 878, Richard du Toit 399, Albert Froneman 107, 572, 751, 775a, 779, 793a, 869, Clem Haagner 56, 121a, 123b, 125a, 126a, 127b, 132a, 132b, 136, 149b, 161a, 162b, 163a, 172a, 179a, 179b, 183b, 186a, 194, 373, 375, 432, 433, 441, 452a, 557, 651, 701a, 735, 741, 810b, Ben Harmse 574, 732a, 834b, Fanie Hendriks 63b, 71b, 95, 97a, 112b, 114a, 146a, 149a, 180b, 182b, 183a, 201, 269, 272, 274, 298, 301, 316, 358, 359a, 363, 377a, 406, 516a, 516b, 528, 547, 548, 566, 586b, 761a, 770, 807a, 807b, 811a, 813a, 814a, 821a, 826a, 826b, 829b, 842a, 845a, 845b, 847, 852a, 852b, 854a, 855b, 856b, 872, 884, 885, 886a, 886b, 887, Lex Hes 21, 281, 657, Johan Knobel 57, 72a, 169a, 481b, Nico Myburgh 141a, 141b, 158a, 162a, 257, 322, 338a, 367, 480, 488a, 587a, 590, 621, 643, 701b, 710a, 879, Louis Nel 512, Ulrich Oberprieler 3a, 3b, 49b, 60a, 71a, 74b, 81, 85, 90b, 92, 94, 97b, 103a, 103b, 104, 105, 112a, 113a, 113b, 115a, 115b, 116a, 121b, 122b, 124, 135b, 142, 143b, 148a, 152b, 158b, 169b, 172b, 182a, 188b, 195, 198a, 203b, 204, 226a, 226b, 238a, 239a, 239b, 244, 258, 260, 264, 266, 284, 312a, 312b, 315a, 315b, 324, 347b, 348a, 349, 352, 356a, 359b, 364, 370, 371, 401, 402, 417, 421, 424, 435b, 437, 438, 451, 452b, 457a, 457b, 458, 460, 515a, 518, 534, 545b, 550, 577b, 593b, 602, 711, 713, 732c, 739, 756, 757b, 760b, 763, 768, 769a, 772, 799b, 811b, 813b, 821b, 824a, 832a, 834a, 844, 846, 857, Photo Access/David Bristow 793a, Photo Access/J J Brooks 425, 498b, 500b, 529, 552, 611, 614, 645, 742, 827, 840, Photo Access/GPL du Plessis 486b, Photo Access/HPH Photography 139, 190, 338b, 454, Photo Access/David Steele 615, Photo Access/Peter Steyn 143a, 192, 523, 667, 688, Veronica Roodt 72b, 447, Peter Steyn 131b, 408, 572, 638, 661, 757a, Warwick Tarboton 180a, 234, 235, 378, 470, 474b, 530, 538a, 582a, 583b, 600, 685a, 698a, 703b, 744, 748, 831, Heinrich van den Berg 774, 810a, Philip van den Berg 65a, 86, 131a, 161b, 165, 345b, 469, 526, 677, 683, Rip van Wyk 140b, 392, 396, 397, 398, Hein von Hörsten 127a, 350, 431, 488b, 596a, 686, 700b, 706, 773a, 773b, 777a, 777b, 783a, 783b, 796a, Lanz von Hörsten 186b, 481a, 551, 554, 596b, 681b, 690, 700a, 746, 785, 862a, Alan Weaving 238b, John Wesson 299, 429a, 689, 698b, 788b, Alan Wilson 8a, 12, 49a, 50, 67, 76a, 91, 108, 213, 228, 240b, 246a, 248, 249, 254, 262, 270, 271, 290, 294, 327a, 327b, 339a, 339 b, 483a, 506b, 524, 533, 648.

New Names

The International Ornithological Committee is currently standardising the common names of birds from all over the world. For this reason some (but not all) established Southern African names have been changed to correspond with international usage. The new names of species described in this pocket-guide are given below:

Old Name		New Name
Barbet	Red-fronted Tinker	Red-fronted Tinkerbird
	Yellow-fronted Tinker	Yellow-fronted Tinkerbird
Bishop	Golden	Yellow-crowned Bishop
Bulbul	African Yellow-bellied	Yellow-bellied Greenbul
	Black-eyed	Dark-capped Bulbul
	Sombre	Sombre Greenbul
Bunting	Cinnamon-breasted Rock	Cinnamon-breasted Bunting
Canary	Yellow-eyed	Yellow-fronted Canary
Chat	Mocking	Mocking Cliff-Chat
	Mountain	Mountain Wheatear
	Southern Ant-eating	Ant-eating Chat
Cisticola	Fan-tailed	Zitting Cisticola
Crane	Southern Crowned	Grey Crowned Crane
Crow	Black	Cape Crow
Cuckoo	Diederik	Diderick Cuckoo
Dabchick	-	Little Grebe
Dikkop	Spotted	Spotted Thick-knee
	Water	Water Thick-knee
Dove	Green-spotted	Emerald-spotted Wood-Dove
Duck	Knob-billed	Comb Duck
Eagle	Black	Verreaux's Eagle
	Black-breasted Snake	Black-chested Snake-Eagle
	Crowned	African Crowned Eagle
Egret	Black	Black Heron
	Great White	Great Egret
Finch	Melba	Green-winged Pytilia
	Quail	African Quailfinch
Finch-lark	Chestnut-backed	Chestnut-backed Sparrowlark
	Grey-backed	Grey-backed Sparrowlark
Firefinch	Blue-billed	African Firefinch
Flycatcher	Dusky	African Dusky Flycatcher
Francolin	Greywing	Grey-winged Francolin
	Red-necked	Red-necked Spurfowl
	Redwing	Red-winged Francolin
	Swainson's	Swainson's Spurfowl
Gallinule	Purple	African Purple Swamphen
Goose	Pygmy	African Pygmy Goose
Goshawk	Pale Chanting	Southern Pale Chanting Goshawk
Grassbird	-	Cape Grassbird
Gull	Kelp	Cape Gull
Gymnogene	-	African Harrier-Hawk
Hornbill	Grey	African Grey Hornbill
Ibis	Sacred	African Sacred Ibis
Kestrel	Eastern Red-footed	Amur Falcon
	Western Red-footed	Red-footed Falcon
Korhaan	Black-bellied	Black-bellied Bustard
	White-quilled	Northern Black Korhaan
Lark	Southern Thick-billed	Large-billed Lark
Longclaw	Orange-throated	Cape Longclaw
Lourie	Grey	Grey Go-away-bird

	Knysna	Knysna Turaco
	Purple-crested	Purple-crested Turaco
Myna	Indian	Common Myna
Oriole	Eastern Black-headed	Black-headed Oriole
Owl	African Barred	African Barred Owlet
	Giant Eagle	Verreaux's Eagle Owl
	Pearl-spotted	Pearl-spotted Owlet
	White-faced	Southern White-faced Scops Owl
Pelican	Eastern White	Great White Pelican
Penguin	Jackass	African Penguin
Pigeon	Feral Pigeon	Rock Dove
	Rameron	African Olive Pigeon
	Rock	Speckled Pigeon
Pipit	Grassveld	African Pipit
Plover	Blacksmith	Blacksmith Lapwing
	Black-winged	Black-winged Lapwing
	Crowned	Crowned Lapwing
	Wattled	African Wattled Lapwing
Robin	African White-throated	White-throated Robin-Chat
	Cape	Cape Robin-Chat
	Heuglin's	White-browed Robin-Chat
	Kalahari	Kalahari Scrub-Robin
	Karoo	Karoo Scrub-Robin
	Natal	Red-capped Robin-Chat
	White-browed	White-browed Scrub-Robin
Shrike	African Long-tailed	Magpie Shrike
	Fiscal	Common Fiscal
	White Helmet	White-crested Helmet-Shrike
Snipe	Ethiopian	African Snipe
Starling	African Pied	Pied Starling
	European	Common Starling
	Glossy	Cape Glossy Starling
	Meve's Long-tailed	Meve's Starling
	Plum-coloured	Violet-backed Starling
Stonechat	Common	African Stonechat
Stork	African Open-billed	African Openbill
Sunbird	African Black	Amethyst
	Lesser Double-collared	Southern Double-collared Sunbird
Swallow	European	Barn Swallow
Tchagra	Three-streaked	Brown-crowned Tchagra
Tit	Southern Grey	Grey Tit
Warbler	African Sedge	Little Rush Warbler
	Cape Reed	Lesser Swamp Warbler
	Great Reed	Greater Reed Warbler
	Green-backed Bleating	Green-backed Camaroptera
Waxbill	Black-cheeked	Black-faced Waxbill
Weaver	Spotted-backed	Village Weaver
Whimbrel	-	Common Whimbrel
Whydah	Paradise	Long-tailed Paradise-Whydah
Widow	Long-tailed	Long-tailed Widowbird
	Red-collared	Red-collared Widowbird
	Red-shouldered	Fan-tailed Widowbird
	White-winged	White-winged Widowbird
	Yellow-rumped	Yellow Bishop
Widow-finch	Purple	Purple Indigobird
	Steel-blue	Village Indigobird
Wood-hoopoe	Red-billed	Green Wood-Hoopoe
	Scimitar-billed	Common Scimitarbill